How to Score Your First Game Job
And What to Expect from the Videogame Industry

by Ben Serviss

Copyright © 2017 Ben Serviss
All rights reserved

First Edition

For more on this book: scoreyourfirstgamejob.com
For more on the author: benserviss.com dashjump.com

A Note on Links

This book contains many links to reference materials. Because websites come and go, in the future some resources may be altered or removed by the time you read this book.

If this is the case for any links you come across in this book, a good way to track down past versions of sites is to search for archived versions at archive.org. You can also let me know of any broken links by tweeting to @benserviss and I'll update them for future editions.

Interviewees

This book contains interviews with numerous game developers sprinkled throughout the text. You can also find the complete interviews with each developer in Appendix B at the end.

The interviewees are:

Evan Berman
Senior Community Manager | Bethesda Softworks
Highlighted Gameography: *Elder Scrolls Online, Quake Champions, Elder Scrolls: Legends, ArcheAge, Defiance, HAWKEN, TERA, Hellgate: London*

Caitlin L. Conner
Lead Narrative Designer | Gameloft
Highlighted Gameography: *The Blacklist: Conspiracy, Dragon Mania Legends, Order and Chaos 2: Redemption*

Dennis Crow
Game Director | Awol
Highlighted Gameography: *World of Warcraft, Grand Theft Auto V*

Nick Madonna
Founder/Business Development | PHL Collective
Highlighted Gameography: *F.E.A.R., TimeShift, Halo: Combat Evolved Anniversary, Tom and Jerry: Colossal Catastrophe, ClusterPuck 99*

John McLean-Foreman
Narrative Director/Lead Writer | Freelance
Highlighted Gameography: *Killzone 3, Splinter Cell: Double Agent, Black & White 2*

Josh Raab
Associate Game Designer | Big Huge Games
Highlighted Gameography: *Nika, Sumer, Crystal Brawl, DomiNations*

Coray Seifert
Director of Production | Experiment 7
Highlighted Gameography: *Magic Table* Series, *Homefront*, *Frontlines: Fuel of War*

Evan Skolnick
Senior Writer | Telltale Games
Highlighted Gameography: *The Walking Dead: A New Frontier*, *Mafia III*, *Gunship Battle 2 VR*, *Star Wars Battlefront*

Neil Sveri
Programmer and Co-Founder | DreamSail Games
Highlighted Gameography: *Don't F**K Up*, *Blade Ballet*

Dylan Tredrea
Product Manager | Rovio
Highlighted Gameography: *Angry Birds Evolution*, *Angry Birds Action*, *Star Wars Assault Team*, *Nemo's Reef*

Raison Varner
Sound Designer and Composer | Gearbox Software
Highlighted Gameography: *Prey*, *Red Faction: Guerrilla*, *Brothers in Arms: Hell's Highway*, *Borderlands*, *Borderlands 2*, *Tales from the Borderlands*, *Aliens: Colonial Marines*, *Battleborn*

Contents

Overview	1
Chapter 1: Before You Begin	3
Nice to Meet You	3
Why Games?	6
Be Informed	7
What Kind of Game Job Do I Want?	7
What If I'm Still Not Sure?	12
Chapter 2: Breaking In	14
Breaking In Is a Process	14
Leveling Up Into Games	15
The Recipe for Success	16
Step 1: Always Be Making Things	16
Group Projects: Practice Working in Teams	26
Finish and Ship	27
Step 2: Get Informed	29
Step 3: Establish an Online Presence	36
Step 4: Make Contacts	44
Why Do I Need People?	44

Where Do I Meet People?	47
But I Live in the Boonies!	48
A Note For the Introverted	49
Advanced Networking Move: Become the Press	50
Step 5: Get Involved	52
Write for Game Sites	52
Volunteer at Conventions	54
Be Helpful to Others	54
Step 6: Display Your Competency and Value	60
Who Am I Impressing?	60
Step 7: Unify Your Messaging	62
Case Study: Business Card	62
Step 8: Apply, Apply, Apply	67
Bonus Step 9: Become an Organizer	69
Bonus Step 10: Learn From the Past	70
Chapter 3: Rites of Passage	**72**
Walk the Path	72
Local Meetups	73
Become a Regular	73
(Optional) Present Something	73
(Optional) Organize Something	74
GGJ: Global Game Jam	76

    Register at a Big Site 78
    Don't Worry 78
    Work With New People 79
    Play the Games, Talk to Devs 80
    (Bonus) Play Games Around the World 81
GDC: The Game Developers Conference 82
    What To Expect 82
    Option One: Volunteer as a CA 85
    Option Two: Get a Student Scholarship 85
    Option Three: Win a Contest 86
    Option Four: Buy a Pass 86
    Option Five: Skip the Pass (Veterans Only) 87
    Optimize Networking for Results 88
    Go to the Parties 90
The Hiring Mindset 93
    Help Them Mitigate Risk 96
Which Do You Do? 97

Chapter 4: You're In - Now What? **98**

Your First Game Job 98
    Make Your Mark, With Eyes Open 99
    Adjust Your Professional Expectations 99
    Above All, Distinguish Yourself 101

Your Second+ Game Job	102
Chapter 5: Conclusion	**107**
Play The Game	107
Acknowledgements	**108**
Appendix A: Gameography	**110**
Appendix B: Game Developer Interviews	**113**

Overview

"Game production is wonderfully challenging, creative, and collaborative work, and after experiencing it for the first time, I was totally hooked."
  —Caitlin L. Conner
  Lead Narrative Designer | Gameloft

Breaking into the game industry is not an easy thing to do. If you're reading this, that means you've decided to seriously pursue turning your hobby into a dream job.

Here's my promise to you: If you're going to take this seriously, so will I. This book contains zero filler material. Everything in this book is here solely to help you get a job in game development. My goal is to transfer everything I've learned and experienced in my journey to the game industry to you.

In Chapter 1: Before You Begin, we'll prepare for the road ahead by assessing your motivations for getting into games and confirming that a career in games is the right choice for you.

In Chapter 2: Breaking In, I'll tell you everything you need to do to break into the game industry.

In Chapter 3: Rites of Passage, I'll walk you through fundamental experiences that nearly everyone who breaks into games goes through, and how to get the most out of them.

Finally, in Chapter 4: You're In - Now What?, we'll go over what to expect once you get your foot in the door with your first game development job and beyond.

Important Note: This book focuses on breaking into existing studios, not how to achieve success on your own as an independent game developer. While there are some similarities between the two, they are different enough to require different approaches.

Let's get started.

Chapter 1: Before You Begin

Nice to Meet You

If you're going to be taking advice from me, it'll probably help to know who I am.

Since 2004 I've worked on 24 game projects for 17 companies across nearly every dimension of the industry, including console shooters, branded Facebook games, military training simulations, educational games, F2P MMOs and text adventures.

Industry Talk
- *F2P*: Short for free-to-play. Games that are free to start playing, but offer in-game purchases in order to make money.
- *MMO*: Short for Massively Multiplayer Online. Genre of game where hundreds or thousands of players can play in the same game world.
- *Gameography*: A list of games that someone has worked on.

I've worked across disciplines as a game designer, producer, product manager, writer and developer, and I also made use of my experience teaching a college class on game design methodologies. For more detail, you can find my full gameography at the end of this book in Appendix A.

While some projects were more successful than others, the key takeaway is that I was able to **consistently break into new sectors of the industry**.

Here's the short version of my experience. See if you can notice the pattern:

Job	Project	How'd I Get It
1. Writing Intern	Online Text-Based Game	Found a company near my college hiring an intern
2. Contract Game Designer	Military Training Simulation	Recommended by a friend
3. Associate Producer	Console FPS	Recommended by a friend
4. Product Manager	F2P MMO	Online job board
5. Contract Game Designer	Educational Game	Recommended by a friend
6. Gamification Designer	Multiple Contract-based Gamification Projects	Job posting on a game industry email group
7. Contract Game Designer	Turn-based Strategy Game	Wrote a blog post on a game industry news site
8. Writer and Developer	Text-Based Multiple Choice Adventure	Met one of the company founders at the Game Developers Conference
(Bonus) Adjunct Lecturer	Game Design College Course Instructor	Recommended by a friend

Industry Talk

- *FPS*: First-person shooter. A game where you play as the first-person perspective of the player character and the primary action is shooting projectiles.
- *Gamification*: An experience that uses aspects of game design in order to elicit a desired behavior. Frequent flier programs are an early example.

Do you see the pattern? You might think that the pattern is having friends who can recommend you for jobs. That's part of it, but there's more.

Was it that every job I got came from actively pursuing game development work? While I was definitely trying my hardest to find jobs, the opportunities that came from recommendations were more passive than active.

Here's the pattern: **Opportunities for game development jobs come from all sorts of places**. The more active you are in seeking them out, the more likely you'll come across one at the precise moment that you are prepared for it.

Why Write This Book?

Getting into games is hard and many people want to do it. Over the years I've received the same email from friends, relatives, and parents, asking for advice on how they or their children can get into games.

I'm happy to help. After all, I was in the same exact position not that long ago. But instead of writing individual replies recommending steps to break into the industry, I realized it would make more sense to condense everything I've learned into something portable, like a book, that can be more thorough than a single email ever could be.

I've also seen the long view of what happens after you break into the industry. When I was starting out, my friends and I were all industry hopefuls. A decade later, some of us have moved on to work on some of the biggest games in the world, start our own ventures and companies, and nurture the next generation to come.

Yet even as technologies, platforms and gaming's place in society change over the years, the underlying elements of the journey to break into games will remain the same. That's what this book is for: to help you navigate through them.

Why Games?

Before you begin the journey to the games industry in earnest, you should have answers to these questions:

1. Why do I want to work in games?
2. Am I prepared for a life working in games?

Why do I want to work in games?

Do you love videogames? Can you think of nothing else that would make you as happy as you would be working on games all day? Do you understand the difference between actively developing games versus playing them for enjoyment? Are you willing to put in the time, effort and energy to break into an extremely competitive industry that is only becoming more so by the day?

Am I prepared for a life working in games?

Are you aware of the reality of working in the game industry? Are you willing and able to relocate to another state, or possibly another country, to find a job? Are you willing to accept a high level of uncertainty and instability in your working life? Game companies often endure waves of layoffs or go out of business. Do you have a support system that can help you during times when work is scarce?

At the same time, the industry is growing and expanding as new platforms and technologies reach bigger audiences. Are you prepared to always be actively managing your career to maximize opportunities? Are you excited to always be learning new things about your chosen discipline and improving your skills?

In general, entry-level pay in the game industry is lower compared to other fields. Are you willing to potentially work for lower wages than for comparable jobs in other industries? Are you aware of the practice of **'crunch' - long periods of overtime work, sometimes unscheduled or unplanned** - that can stretch for weeks or months at a time? Are you willing to work the crunch hours needed to ship a project without a guarantee of additional compensation?

Be Informed

The above is not meant to scare you. It is meant to impart an accurate picture of what the average game developer's life is like.

If you're willing to live with these conditions in order to make games for a living, great. Be informed and reach for your dream. However, if you are not, perhaps there are other paths you would be happier pursuing. If you have a spouse or family and the idea of potential relocation is not an option, it's understandable that the game development lifestyle may put additional constraints on the kinds of jobs you can shoot for.

If you're not sure, you can always give games a chance and see what you think. Life's too short to not try bringing your dreams to fruition if you have the means, aptitude and motivation.

What Kind of Game Job Do I Want?

If you're not sure what exactly you want to do in games, it can be intimidating trying to figure out how you could contribute. Even if you already know you want to be an artist or programmer, it can be daunting figuring out exactly what people who work in those capacities do on a day-to-day basis.

Here's a general breakdown of the different disciplines you can pick from, with some examples of specific jobs within each area. Note that depending on the size of the studio, some of these jobs may be performed by one person or shared by a few developers.

A Note on Game Design Jobs
If your goal is to become a game designer, you will most likely need to become familiar with programming concepts, scripting workflows, level editors, Excel formulas, and data-driven design concepts.

The actual work that goes into game design can be surprisingly technical and the better understanding you have of these ideas, the easier it'll be to implement your designs into the game itself. You don't need to become a full-on programmer, but don't let yourself get too intimidated to stretch yourself in developing your skills.

Programming
Good for: People who like solving puzzles, organizing things and being in control
You might be: Patient, curious, determined, inventive, mathematically-inclined

Sample jobs:

- **Systems Programmers** implement game mechanics and improve how the game plays.
- **Network Programmers** implement online systems for multiplayer features.
- **Graphics Programmers** implement visual assets designed by artists and animators.

Industry Talk
- *Game Mechanics*: The underlying rules of how the game works. For example, one of the main gameplay mechanics in the original *Super Mario Brothers* is the ability to jump. In the first Zelda game *The Legend of Zelda*, one of the main mechanics is the sword attack.

Art
Good for: People who value creative expression, visual design and emotion
You might be: Artistically-inclined, intuitive, visionary

Sample jobs:

- **Concept Artists** create images illustrating a game world's characters, places and moods to help the rest of the team flesh out their part of the project.
- **Illustrators** create lots of images used throughout a game, from logos and avatars to production art for in-game brands and products.
- **UI Designers** create the menus and in-game interface elements players user to interact with the game.
- **Animators** bring 2D and 3D figures to life in gameplay and cinematic sequences.
- **3D Artists** sculpt 3D characters and figures for everything in a game, from player characters to buildings to vehicles.

Game Design

Good for: People who like mastering the rules, improving processes and asking questions
You might be: Full of ideas, inquisitive, interested in how people think, intrigued by math

Sample jobs:

- **Scripters** plan and implement gameplay events that happen in a level.
- **Level Designers** design and lay out individual levels in 2D and 3D level editor programs.
- **Systems Designers** design rulesets and core mechanics for how games work.

Production

Good for: People who like organizing events, thinking ahead and fixing problems
You might be: Flexible, good with people, outgoing, punctual, self-directed

Sample jobs:

- **Project Managers** organize the day-to-day process of creating a game, broken out into different phases.

- **Product Managers** act as the CEO of a game or game feature, working across all disciplines to research and identify the best decisions for the project.
- **Producers** manage project schedules, work within the company as a whole to keep the project moving, work with external groups to fulfill development needs, and do anything else needed to keep the game on track and the team unblocked.

One thing to note is that producer roles can vary from company to company. For example, at one studio, the producers might manage the schedule, while at another, they might drive specific game features, workflows, or contribute to creative decisions.

Audio
Good for: People who love playing with sound, noticing how sound affects experiences and puzzling out how things work
You might be: Able to play multiple instruments, fond of singing, hyper-aware of audio in movies, TV and games

Sample jobs:

- **Sound Designers** create sound effects for everything you'd hear in a game, from menu clicks and beeps to explosions and ambient background noise, as well as design systems that play back audio during gameplay in a natural, non-repetitive way. They may also record and source sound effects from physical materials in the studio and in the field.
- **Composers** create both stand-alone songs for scripted sequences as well as modular song components that can be re-arranged in real-time to complement events as you play.

Sound Design vs Composition
In today's game industry, composers are almost exclusively contracted on a project basis, and are rarely employed as full-time in-house employees. If you want to get a full-time job in game audio, focus on preparing yourself for sound design positions. Only aim for work as a

composer if you're willing and able to pursue a freelance career as a contractor.

Quality Assurance (QA)
Good for: People who like figuring out how things work, investigating mysteries and asking why
You might be: Detail-oriented, curious, self-directed, a bit of a rebel

Sample jobs:

- **Game Testers** play through the game in a half-finished state and try to break the game in order to find bugs for the development team to fix.
- **QA Managers** manage groups of testers for different projects, create schedules and help the test team meet their goals.
- **Technical Requirements Testers** evaluate games for compliance with mandatory technical requirements from console manufacturers (eg. Sony, Microsoft, Nintendo) so that finished games will be accepted by the console manufacturer to be published.

Writing
Good for: People who like telling stories and using language and who are interested in human behavior
You might be: A bookworm, deeply affected by stories, empathetic, thoughtful

Sample jobs:

- **Game Writers** write a multitude of things for games, including high-level story design, in-game dialog, menu and manual text, audio logs, item descriptions, press materials and more.
- **Scriptwriters** write both in-game and pre-rendered cinematics that move the game's narrative forward.
- **Narrative Designers** work with the development team to create gameplay systems that complement a game's minute-to-minute and overarching narrative goals.

Community Management
Good for: People who like writing, introducing new concepts to people, and enjoy social media
You might be: Able to read a room, the life of the party, enthusiastic, self-starting

Sample jobs:

- **Community Managers** directly communicate with a game's fanbase, alert the developers about player concerns, and help get players excited about upcoming features.
- **Social Media Managers** plan and publish updates on a game's social media channels to help spread awareness about the game and get current and prospective players excited to play.

What If I'm Still Not Sure?

"I thought I decided what I wanted to do quite early in my career but that ended up evolving and taking different forms over time. My initial thought was to break in as an environment artist but that soon changed after I got into QA. I got a bulk of my experience in management from QA onward into Production. My critical path diverged from art into QA into production into studio management – and that's the simple version."
—*Nick Madonna*
Founder/Business Development | PHL Collective

After going through those categories, there are probably a few that already jump out at you. If so, that's great. Explore those disciplines of game development as you start to get more familiar with the industry.

If you still think that there is no clear-cut fit for you, that's OK. It's widely accepted that game testers and assistant or associate producer positions are good entry-level jobs to aim for when breaking in, regardless of the path you decide to pursue.

Once you get in the door and are able to learn more about game development from the inside, you'll find opportunities to refine your skills and eventually transition over to your chosen discipline once you identify it.

A Note on Starting Out in Game Testing
If you decide to go this route, be prepared to spend a few years learning how to be an effective tester and refining your skills in your desired field before you get the chance to apply for something in that field.

Along those same lines, be aware that some larger companies take active steps to separate development and QA teams to prevent testers from jumping (or repeatedly attempting to jump) into development. After all, studios need functioning QA departments to properly test their games. If everyone leaves QA, that would be pretty bad for the project!

Another thing to consider is that getting experience as a game tester can help when you apply for entry-level development positions at other studios. So remember that if your current company discourages you from moving from test to development, that experience can still help you later.

Chapter 2: Breaking In

"I think the biggest roadblock for people trying to get into the industry is their own apprehension. I've met plenty of people with the excuse of 'I just don't know how to start'. The best way to start is to start."
 —*Neil Sveri*
 Programmer and Co-Founder | DreamSail Games

Breaking In Is a Process

Spoiler: Breaking into the games industry is not something you do once, but a continual process. It is a collection of actions you take until you look around and realize that someone is paying you to make games.

It's certainly possible to blindly apply for a job without any relevant experience or connections, but the odds are extremely low of anything coming of it.

Even after you've gotten into the game industry, you may find yourself having to break in all over again depending on how a given job turns out. For example, if the studio where you've been working for the past year suddenly loses its funding and closes down, you may find that your job search feels awfully like breaking in the first time. Fortunately, the advice in this book will work just as well for these additional times.

A crucial component of breaking into games is networking - meeting game developers, game industry hopefuls, and anyone else involved in the games business. We'll go over this in greater detail later in this section. In the meantime, get ready to make a whole lot of new friends.

Question: Say, for example, there are only three ways to break into the game industry. One of them takes a significant amount of time, one of them costs a non-trivial amount of money (whatever that means to you), and one of them requires serious self-improvement. Which of them do you do?

Got your answer? Hang on to it. We'll be back to answer it later.

Leveling Up Into Games

As you break into games, you'll move through three distinct stages.

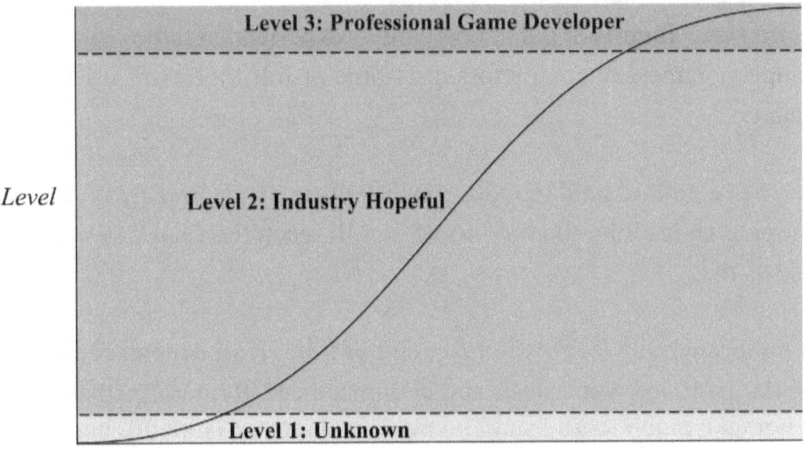

Time & Effort

Level 1: Unknown
Who are they? Gamers, students, people who are thinking about breaking into games

The Unknown group covers people who are completely unknown to anybody involved in the games business in any way. The first step to breaking in involves moving out of this group and into the next level. Fortunately, this is not too hard to do.

Level 2: Industry Hopeful
Who are they? Students, people at game development meetups, brand new indie developers, people working on game side projects who have not shipped a game

You've made some contacts with other industry hopefuls, and maybe even a game developer or two. You've got a presence on social media and an online portfolio. You may no longer be a complete stranger to the game development community, but you're not in the industry yet.

Moving on to the next and final level takes the longest, so remember to be patient.

Level 3: Professional Game Developer
Who are they? Interns at game companies, experienced indie developers, game dev contractors, part-time or full-time staff at game companies

Once you're getting paid to make games, either by a company or by developing and selling them yourself, you'll reach the final level. It's as simple as that.

Moving through the levels can take a lot of time. It all depends on your particular path, interests, skills and circumstances. Remember that it does not take much to go from Unknown to Industry Hopeful, but it requires a lot of work and effort to reach the third stage.

Above all, be patient with yourself. Try your best to enjoy the journey.

The Recipe for Success

Earlier we established that breaking into the game industry is a process. Here is how that process works.

Step 1: Always Be Making Things

"The single best way to communicate your value to veteran game developers is to be always making things."
    —*Raison Varner*
    Sound Designer and Composer | Gearbox Software

This is the most critical aspect of getting into game development. Nothing compares to presenting actual concrete work when talking to professional game devs or other industry hopefuls. You must always be making things.

While finished games and demos are the ideal thing to make, don't worry if you're not a programmer. Game design documents, storyboards, concept art, demo reels, demo tracks, blog posts - there is always something you could be working on regardless of what discipline you choose to pursue.

This list gives an overview of some things you can make, in descending order of priority.

1. A finished game

This is the best possible scenario. If you're looking for a game job and can point to a game you've made yourself, that's a huge indication that you can literally do the work.

However, intending to complete and ship your first-ever game project is commonly understood to be a mistake. Developing and finishing a game is surprisingly difficult, and will require you to learn an immense amount about all the critical details required to release a finished game that you may not have thought about - in addition to already being knowledgeable and experienced in game development.

Instead of leaping into things head-first, start with a smaller project focusing on your chosen discipline. Only when you're able to finish projects of increasing scope will it be time to tackle creating a finished game. You can also team up with friends on projects, though it's best to wait until you've obtained a measure of familiarity with your chosen discipline so you can contribute meaningfully.

Industry Talk
- *Scope*: The size of something. The scope of a gigantic game like *Skyrim* is big, while choose-your-own-adventure-style text games have a smaller scope. Projects that have had too many features added to them can be described as "over-scoped."

"Early in your career, you need to create at a ferocious pace. It might not be perfect, because you're just starting out. If you're extremely talented or lucky, you may end up working on something great. If you don't, that's fine. Going through the process of creating anything will set you miles apart from the mass of people who are afraid to get their hands dirty with something less than their perfect vision of what a game is. Get out there and create anything while constantly striving to get better at your craft. The quality will come with time and repetition."
    —Coray Seifert
    Director of Production | Experiment 7

You also aren't ever required to have a complete game in your portfolio. Plenty of game developers start off with portfolios of demos or other kinds of proof-of-concept pieces that help them get jobs, and after they ship games in a professional capacity, their work on released products can speak for their abilities. While it's certainly impressive to have a finished game in your portfolio, don't feel like it's an absolute must.

Done Is Better Than Long
When creating your own games, always prioritize completing the project over game length. Having completed two small games that can be finished by the player in 15 minute play sessions is vastly preferable to not finishing one game that will have 20 playable hours.

Reference Material [Playable]
I developed a short text-based game in GameMaker both as a portfolio piece and as an exercise in non-linear narrative. While this game definitely won't win any awards, it did help me get contract jobs as a game writer.

Download *I Am Trying to Tell You Something (Win)* http://www.dashjump.com/files/IAmTryingtoTellYouSomething.zip

2. A playable demo

Having something in any kind of playable format is a good indication of your abilities and drive. Your demo can certainly be rough, but make sure that it's impressive in some way. If there's an innovative game mechanic, great. If your hand-animated characters look fantastic, awesome. If you're not sure if your demo is ready to show people, ask some friends for their honest feedback.

Reference Material [Playable]
Some sample playable demos:

Gustav Dahl, *Super Globe Dash*
http://gustavdahl.net/super-globe-dash

Molly Jameson, *Trendy Tech CEO*
http://www.mollyjameson.com/personalprojects
http://www.kongregate.com/games/UltraRat/trendy-tech-ceo

Nina Freedman, *how do you Do It?*
http://ninasays.so/howdoyoudoit

Leanne C. Taylor-Giles, Story Moments
http://www.leannectaylor.com/story-moments.html

"One of the biggest motivators for my work is learning, so a lot of my practice would just be to answer a single question like 'How do projectiles work?'."
　　—*Neil Sveri*
　　Programmer and Co-Founder | DreamSail Games

3. Gameplay video/non-playable demo

Even if people can't play it, having a short video or non-playable demo is a good way to quickly show off what you can do. Stick to gameplay footage and don't bother with a consumer-oriented trailer, unless you're focusing on cinematics or marketing as your path.

Make sure you don't rely on Ken Burns-style panning over concept art to get the point across, as that technique often indicates you're still early in the planning stages and don't have much to show yet.

Reference Material [Portfolio]
Julein Lebon, *The Blob Minute*
julienlebon.com/#/portfolio/blob-minute-game-design-level-design

Wade Henricksen, Highlight Reel
http://darktreemedia.com/highlights

4. Game art

This can be anything that qualifies as game art. In-game character illustrations, concept art, animations, 3D renders; pretty much any kind of art that goes into a game is fair play.

Reference Material [Portfolio]
Christoffer Radsby's portfolio
http://christofferradsby.com

Seth Nash's portfolio
http://www.sethnash.com

Game Art Portfolio Wall
http://gameartportfoliowall.com

5. Demo reels (for sound designers)

Be prepared to create two video demo reels: one focused on in-game sound design, and another on cinematic design.

Your in-game demo needs to sound like a game. Ideally, this will actually just consist of game captures of projects you worked on. But if not, remember that while you're working in a DAW (digital audio workstation), your goal is to have your audio sound like it's triggered from within a game, not a cinematic. In other words, you're not designing a cinematic soundscape over in-game footage. Save that for your cinematic reel.

The cinematic reel is where you demonstrate your talent and knowledge of traditional post mixing. In many respects the in-game demo reel will be more important, especially if it's composed of direct game footage.

A Note for Composers
If you're focusing on composition, the best expectation to form is that you will be dealing with challenges unique to operating as an independent contractor instead of an in-house, salaried employee. You will most likely live a freelance lifestyle. This is a whole separate topic that requires a book of its own. This book focuses mostly on an in-house development track.

While there are a few in-house composer positions here and there throughout the industry, the lion's share of work is handled by freelance media composers. This is true even in the indie developer marketplace. If you intend to work as an in-house developer, and you still wish to do music, you will need to also become a great sound designer and be prepared to present your sound design credentials first because the dedicated composer positions just aren't as numerous as they used to be.

In general, understand that these two short demos need to communicate your range and depth of knowledge within a short time frame. It's also not unusual for years of material to be needed before you have materials of sufficient quality, or you create your final demo. In other words, this is a long-term project and it probably won't be done by the time you leave school. Some people get lucky and get in quick, but many more do not.

The purpose of these videos is to express your creativity as a sound designer through the originality and fidelity of your content. The goal is to accomplish that in under two minutes. In addition to that, bear in mind that if you don't capture the reviewer's interest within the first 10 seconds, you can't be sure that the rest was seen. You might get lucky and the reviewer might skip through the video and have their interest captured then, but if the quality of the demo isn't top-notch within the first 10 seconds, you should assume that reviewers will have moved to the next in the stack.

Reference Material [Portfolio]
Mattia Cellotto, Meet the Pyro Sound Redesign http://www.mattiacellotto.com/portfolio/meet-the-pyro-sound-redesign

Andrew Shcherbak, Game Audio Showreel
www.pencilboxsounds.com/?project=project-1-img

Brian Ploof, Demo Reel 2013
http://www.bryanploof.com

"I made sure that every project I worked on, I took away one great screenshot, game design document, or scriptwriting sample. Prospective employers liked that I had the initiative to find a team, learn new tech, and finish anything, even if it was not quite at AAA level yet."
—Coray Seifert
Director of Production | Experiment 7

6. Writing samples

There are plenty of avenues to showcase your game writing skills. Come up with a hypothetical game project and put together some example content for different needs.

For example, say your example game is an open world adventure game similar to later entries in the *Far Cry* series.

You can:

- Write a sample cinematic to showcase your dialog and pacing skills.

- Write sample descriptions for items that would appear in the player's inventory screen.
- Write character bios for main characters in the game.
- Write a high-level breakdown for a section of gameplay, tying together level and gameplay goals to narrative stakes.
- Write sample "barks" for AI characters for common gameplay situations, like "I spotted the player" or "I'm low on ammo."

Reference Material [Portfolio]
Matt Fleming, Writing Samples
http://flemingme.com/?cat=6

Jonathon Myers, Narrative Game Samples
http://www.jonathonmyers.com/narrative-game-samples.html

Shirley Park, Writing Samples
https://www.parkpage14.com/writing-samples

Industry Talk
- *Cinematic*: A non-interactive segment in the game, commonly used to convey narrative elements. Also known as a cut-scene.
- *Narrative Stakes*: The main source of tension in building an effective narrative. The possible positive or negative outcomes of something in a narrative.
- *Barks*: Short lines of dialog game characters say to convey information to the player.

7. Design documents

The industry has been moving away from gigantic all-in-one game design documents or GDDs, largely because nobody on the dev team reads them once production begins, but smaller design documents are still useful in the development process.

You can:

- Write a high-level pitch doc outlining the premise of your example game, identifying the target market, explaining the platform and tech decisions, etc.
- Write docs outlining the mechanics for your example game in detail. Show your level of thought behind your decisions. You can also focus on just one game mechanic if you don't want to skimp out on details while keeping the doc to a readable length.
- Write a doc walking through every aspect of a sample level. Describe the level layout and progression, characters/enemies encountered, mechanics, visual/audio assets needed, etc. Make it as complete as possible while staying brief and interesting.
- Write a one-pager outlining the game from a high level, describing its features, the team required, the target platforms, estimated development time and competing games.

Here's some good additional reference material for putting together game design docs:

Reference Material [Reading]
This lengthy article on gametuts.com goes into the details of what you might want to include in a game design document.
https://code.tutsplus.com/articles/effectively-organize-your-games-development-with-a-game-design-document--active-10140

This GDD for 2009's *Damnation* is a good example of a streamlined game design document intended for pitching to publishers.
https://jacobminkoff.files.wordpress.com/2010/02/damnationextended-web.pdf

This GDD template, hosted publicly on Google Docs, offers a simple structure to get you started.
https://docs.google.com/document/d/1ct5-qyUZC9cAKn-iLUgtOczDkERmPzNNwPLDfT9Hgjs/preview#heading=h.247b8039vfys

8. Blog posts

Write about an aspect of your chosen discipline that fascinates you. Study what's been done before and analyze why it works - or doesn't. Identify trends in game development that nobody's thought of before. Show people the level of your insight.

Reference Material [Reading]
Some examples:

A look at the practice of crunch, excessively long work hours for a temporary period of time, in game development.
http://www.gamasutra.com/view/news/272259/Youre_crunching_So_now_what.php

An in-depth look at the history and evolution of camera systems in games. This post is incredibly thorough, technical and academic. You don't need to get into this level of detail to create a worthwhile blog post, but putting in this amount of effort will certainly make people pay attention.
http://www.gamasutra.com/blogs/ItayKeren/20150511/243083/Scroll_Back_The_Theory_and_Practice_of_Cameras_in_SideScrollers.php

A step-by-step walkthrough of the process of creating a level in Valve's Source engine.
http://magnarj.net/article_workflow.html

Bonus: For added effect, you can syndicate your blog posts on Gamasutra.com by opening an account and setting up a member blog. If Gamasutra's editors think your post is particularly good they'll feature it on their site, which is a great way to get people reading your material and learning about you. If you do go this route, make sure to include links back to your website at the top of your Gamasutra blog post.

Industry Talk
- *Game Engine*: The underlying program used to run a game. Much like how most PCs run Windows and most Macs run MacOS, every game is

powered by an engine. Valve uses its own Source engine for its games, while some companies license engines from other companies so they don't have to create and maintain one themselves.

9. Other writing

Reviews, previews, interviews, features, criticism - any other kind of game writing is fair game for the portfolio as long as it demonstrates your value.

Note that these pieces are best used if you're aiming to break in as a game journalist or critic. If you're looking to break in as a developer, these pieces can still be useful as something to have on your site as you work on more development-focused materials.

Remember the number one rule of getting into games: Always be making things. If you're not constantly doing this, seriously reconsider if getting into games is the right thing for you.

Group Projects: Practice Working in Teams

"Make mods with friends. It was actually a horrible process and it's a miracle our friendships survived, but it was where I got a lot of rookie mistakes out of the way. It also undoubtedly gave me 'street cred' when applying to real game studios without any 'real' shipped games for positions that required game dev experience."
   —*Dylan Tredrea*
   Product Manager | Rovio

As you get started, almost all of your projects will be solo. Once you meet more fellow aspiring game devs, you'll encounter opportunities to work on team projects, whether at game jams or on projects in your spare time.

These projects are invaluable. While you may not be happy with the quality of the finished product, or you may not even complete it, the added experience of working with other people to develop a game is one of the most important skill-building activities you can do. All game studios require collaboration in order to produce a finished game, and like anything else, learning how to develop a game with other people is a skill you will need to learn.

Working on group projects in your spare time, where the consequences for failure are almost nothing, is an excellent way to build up the kind of experience studios require.

Finish and Ship

"The point is to go through the process and finish something so you learn, harshly, how incredibly difficult the process of game development is and how incredibly worthless ideas alone are."
—*Dylan Tredrea*
Product Manager | Rovio

Having something to show, even if it's unfinished, is great. But the most valuable kind of projects to show people are the finished kind.

Finishing a game takes a lot of hard work. It's very easy to come up with a cool idea for a game and start working on it, but it's incredibly difficult to see that vision through to completion and get it out the door. Even a small solo game can take six months to two years to complete, depending on its scope.

Estimate Your Side Project's Development Time
Got an idea for a cool solo game project? Here's a quick way to get a feel for a realistic estimate to finishing it. First, take into account all of the pre-production work, planning, learning new tools, prototyping, playtesting, iterating, polishing, and finalizing that you think it'll take. How long do you think this project will take you?

With that time frame in mind, cut the scope of the game in half and double your initial estimate. This is a realistic estimate to work with.

As you work on projects, focus on finishing one small deliverable at a time - a drawing, a concept for a level, a passage of writing, a song, etc. The key thing is to pick projects that you can complete within a reasonable amount of time as finishing things is more important than producing perfection at this stage.

Industry Talk
- *Deliverable*: A unit of complete work, usually agreed-upon beforehand. For example, if you're an artist working on a 2D character, a deliverable may be a complete walk cycle animation, or it may be a set of portraits to be used as avatars.

Project Management Tools
Here are some handy tools to help manage your projects:

- *Trello is a very versatile tool for managing tasks for small projects.*
- *Slack is a great way to keep in touch with collaborators.*
- *Screenhero is a very useful tool for sharing your screen when working with remote collaborators. There's also a handy Slack integration.*

Staying motivated may be its own challenge. If a project seems to drag on endlessly, think about ways you can simplify it. Remember to keep the long view in mind, and think about what the finished product will eventually look like. Try to focus on enjoying the process of the work itself instead of racing toward the end.

Being able to finish a project in your chosen field (and presumably in your spare time) is a huge indicator that you are capable and mature enough to finish what you start. That quality is one of the most important things in game development.

Step 2: Get Informed

"I read a lot every day. From game press to industry sites and everything in between, I set aside a good portion of my day to keeping up-to-date."
—*Nick Madonna*
Founder/Business Development | PHL Collective

Once you start paying attention to the game industry, you'll start to learn more about the people and companies behind the scenes of your favorite games. If you want to eventually join their ranks, then you'll need to get in the habit of reading about the industry that you're set on entering.

Build up your knowledge base of people, projects, studios, technologies and trends. The goal here is not to have an encyclopedic understanding of all things in the entire universe of game development, but to be familiar with any major topic that might come up in an industry-related discussion. The more apparent it is that you are familiar and comfortable with the game industry as a whole, the easier it will be to convey that you know what you're talking about.

You'll want to:

- Read about industry news so you have an idea of how the business works.
- Read about major figures in the game industry - celebrity developers, the publishing big shots, up and coming industry players, indie breakout stars, and more - so you have a sense of who's important to know and know about.
- Read blog posts by developers to improve your understanding of the development process, even outside your chosen discipline.
- Find groups and communities that focus on discussion of your chosen discipline so you can learn from those who do what you aspire to do.

Here are some resources to get you going:

Reference Material [Reading]

General Game Development

Gamasutra. Gamasutra is the biggest and most well-known game industry news source there is. Read it every day.
http://www.gamasutra.com

Gamesindustry.biz. Gamesindustry.biz has a more business-focused slant toward industry news, which makes it a helpful companion to Gamasutra.
http://www.gamesindustry.biz

Polygon. Polygon's games coverage straddles industry knowledge and consideration for the consumer's perspective, making it a well-rounded source for info.
http://www.polygon.com

GDC Vault. Every year, a big chunk of the talks in the Game Developers Conference (GDC) series of conventions get recorded and put online in the GDC Vault. You usually need to have purchased a pass for that year's conference to view the talks, though GDC makes some of them available to stream free of charge. Check out these free talks for a wealth of knowledge about all kinds of game development disciplines.
http://www.gdcvault.com/free

Double Fine Adventure! When Double Fine kickstarted their adventure game *Broken Age* in 2013, they started releasing backer-exclusive videos documenting the development process. Now that the game has been released, they opened up the entire documentary to the public. DFA is an extremely informative and entertaining look at what game development on a small, but highly visible team really looks like.
https://www.youtube.com/playlist?list=PLIhLvue17Sd7F6pU2ByRRb0igiI-WKk3D

/r/themakingofgames. This subreddit is a good resource of a ton of varied information about the making of all kinds of video games you might have played.
https://www.reddit.com/r/TheMakingOfGames

TIGSource. Aka The Indie Game Source, TIGSource is home to a hopping community of indie game developers. Hang out, ask questions, and soak up what you can.

https://www.tigsource.com
https://forums.tigsource.com

IGDA SIGs (Special Interest Groups). The IGDA (International Game Developers Association) hosts quite a few special interest groups dedicated to different disciplines of game development. Check this list for an inventory of currently active groups.
https://www.igda.org/?page=sigs

Game Career Guide. This site is a reliable source of good information on getting started in game development.
http://www.gamecareerguide.com

GDC State of the Game Industry Report. This free white paper was put together based on input from developers at the Game Developers Conference in 2016. Keep an eye out for newer editions if this becomes outdated.
http://reg.techweb.com/GDCSF17-StateOfGame

> "The best way to stay apprised of trends and avoid fads is to listen: to LinkedIn feeds, to your peers, and to your community."
> —Evan Berman
> Senior Community Manager | Bethesda Softworks

Game Design

The Art of Game Design: A Book of Lenses by Jesse Schell. Schell's book is widely cited as an excellent game design companion, and for good reason. He examines the art and discipline of game design from multiple perspectives and always with a practical eye.
https://www.amazon.com/Art-Game-Design-Lenses-Second/dp/1466598646

Rules of Play: Game Design Fundamentals by Katie Salen Tekinbaş and Eric Zimmerman. This book takes a more theoretical approach to core game design fundamentals.
https://www.amazon.com/Rules-Play-Design-Fundamentals-Press/dp/0262240459

World of Level Design. Lots of resources for learning how to use level editors to craft game levels.
http://worldofleveldesign.com

The Art of Screenshake. This talk by Jan Willem Nijman of Vlambeer dives into the importance of getting the details right when it comes to game feel.
https://www.youtube.com/watch?v=AJdEqssNZ-U

Gamasutra Game Design Articles. There is an enormous wealth of game design wisdom at Gamasutra. A good starting place is their game design deep dives.
http://www.gamasutra.com/deepdives

Art/Visual Design

SIGGRAPH. A loose acronym for Special Interest Group on Computer Graphics and Interactive Techniques, SIGGRAPH is also a conference that focuses on digital visual art and techniques.
http://www.siggraph.org

Learning To Draw Game Characters. This blog post from Big Fish goes through the basics of creating characters intended for use in games.
http://www.bigfishgames.com/blog/learning-to-draw-game-characters

How To Make A Kickass Game Art Portfolio. This post on moddb.com walks through some best practices for putting together an illustration portfolio.
http://www.moddb.com/tutorials/how-to-make-a-kickass-game-art-portfolio

"Twitter is a great resource. It provides a constant source of inspiration, news, and discussion from a large community of game developers. Sites like Gamasutra, Polycount, and TIGsource often link industry news and tutorials. I also like to join IRC and Slack groups for certain things, like a Unity Engine chat or a group for tech artists. They provide front-line news and somewhat intimate access to industry developers."
　—*Neil Sveri*
　Programmer and Co-Founder | DreamSail Games

Audio/Sound Design/Composition

G.A.N.G. (Game Audio Network Guild). A global community for people who work in game audio.
http://www.audiogang.org

IASIG (Interactive Audio Special Interest Group). An organization for people who work in interactive audio, not limited to games.
https://www.iasig.org

FB Group: Video Game - Composers & Sound Designers. A Facebook group for game audio professionals as well as fans.
https://www.facebook.com/groups/2541910980

Creative Field Recording. A blog focused on making live recordings out in the world to be used in the studio.
http://www.creativefieldrecording.com

Designing Sound. A blog dedicated to the art and technique of sound design.
http://designingsound.org

Audio Kinetic's blog. A community for audio professionals to share thoughts, ideas and information.
http://blog.audiokinetic.com

FMOD's site. FMOD is a commonly used audio content creation tool used in commercial games. Their site includes many educational and informational resources.
http://www.fmod.org

Programming/Engineering

Game Engine Documentation & Tutorials. Getting familiar with game engines will be an incredibly useful use of your time, since these are the technologies programmers use on a daily basis to make games. Check out documentation, tutorials and YouTube how-to videos for Unity, Unreal, CRYENGINE and others to help you get your bearings as you experiment with what's possible in game engines.

Unity Documentation: https://docs.unity3d.com/Manual/index.html
Unreal Engine Documentation: https://docs.unrealengine.com/latest/INT
CRYENGINE Documentation: http://docs.cryengine.com/display/SDKDOC1/Home

3D Math Primer For Graphics and Game Development. A good all-around resource for 3D programming.
https://www.amazon.com/Primer-Graphics-Development-Wordware-Library/dp/1556229119

"I talk to friends, play games, and check blogs like Gamasutra. I also read a lot of non-game development books, where I learn a lot about life and human behavior that often can be applied to games and life in general."
—Dennis Crow
Game Director | Awol

Production

So You Want My Job: Video Game Producer. An interview with game producer John E. Williamson.
http://www.artofmanliness.com/2010/09/29/so-you-want-my-job-video-game-producer

What Makes a Good Game Producer? Part 1. Blizzard's Ernst ten Bosch's two-part article series on Gamasutra goes into what it takes to make it as a producer.
http://www.gamasutra.com/blogs/ErnstTenBosch/20130912/200168/What_Makes_a_Good_Game_Producer_Part_1.php

Writing/Narrative Design

IGDA Game Writing Special Interest Group Google Group. The IGDA's Writing SIG (Special Interest Group) has put out books together, held sessions at GDC for years, and has an active Google Group. All you have to do is apply to join:
https://groups.google.com/forum/#!forum/wsig-main

Story: Substance, Structure, Style and the Principles of Screenwriting by Robert McKee. McKee's book focuses on screenplays, but its lessons about story structure apply to all story-based media.
https://www.amazon.com/Story-Substance-Structure-Principles-Screenwriting/dp/0060391685

For Aspiring Games Writers. Game writer Leanne C. Taylor-Giles has put together a great shortlist of recommended reading and steps for getting started as a game writer.
http://www.leannectaylor.com/for-aspiring-games-writers.html

Community Management

CMX Hub. This public Facebook group is dedicated to helping community professionals in all industries thrive.
https://www.facebook.com/groups/cmxhub

Breaking Into the Industry: Jessica Merizan, Bioware Community Manager. This interview sheds light on one CM's journey to working at Bioware.
http://www2.ea.com/news/breaking-into-the-industry-jessica-merizan

What it's like to manage a gaming community on fire. This PC Gamer article chronicles the more intense side of community management.
http://www.pcgamer.com/what-its-like-to-manage-a-gaming-community-on-fire/

Step 3: Establish an Online Presence

Now that you have some projects in the works and you're starting to get a feel for the industry, it's time to dip your toes into it.

Creating an online presence for yourself is a must. Here's how to do it.

1. Make a LinkedIn profile

LinkedIn is a huge social network geared toward professional activity, and if you don't have a profile, make one. The game industry was one of the first industries to heartily adopt LinkedIn and you'll be able to find almost anyone in the industry there. Having a profile page is just another way you can let prospective employers and collaborators find you.

Important Note: Once you're set up with a profile, **do not send invitations to connect to anyone you haven't actually met in real life**. If you send blind invites to developers at your favorite studios and they don't know you, they will delete them. Spamming developers won't get you closer to a job - in fact, it'll only annoy them. Be considerate and deliberate with social media.

For more tips specifically related to LinkedIn, check out this guide:

Reference Material [Reading]
How to Create a Killer LinkedIn Profile That Will Get You Noticed
https://www.linkedin.com/pulse/how-create-killer-linkedin-profile-get-you-noticed-bernard-marr

2. Get on Twitter

If LinkedIn is where everyone works, Twitter is where everyone hangs out. Create a Twitter account, but before you start tweeting away, learn how to use it.

Twitter is an exceptional tool for reaching out to game devs, peers, potential mentors and industry contacts but only **if you know how to use it correctly**. Just like with LinkedIn above, don't spam famous developers or people who work for your favorite companies.

Start slowly, until you have a feel for it. Twitter gaffes aren't the worst thing in the world, but you want to come across as someone competent who adds value.

Stay Out of Political/Social Debates
Don't use any professional social media accounts to jump into political or social debates. It's an incredibly bad idea if you're trying to present yourself as a professional. If you need to participate in these kinds of discussions, do it using a separate account that doesn't have any of your publicly available information.

Note that posting level-headed political statements is not the same as taking part in political debate. Staying silent in today's charged political climate is going to be a difficult prospect. Just make sure to avoid political arguments and don't let your emotions get the best of you in any online venue.

Find some game companies you know and follow their accounts. Then, find game developers with large Twitter followings, follow them, and watch how they use it.

If you're brand new to Twitter, this guide does a good job of walking you through the basics:

Reference Material [Reading]
Mom This Is How Twitter Works
http://www.momthisishowtwitterworks.com

3. Make a portfolio site

The exact specifics of what to put on your site will depend on your chosen discipline, but regardless of your specialty you absolutely need to have your own online portfolio.

Here are some options for getting portfolios up and running:

Reference Material [Tools]
For Everybody

tumblr. Good for artists and displaying visual materials.
https://www.tumblr.com

Carbonmade. Good for lots of different disciplines. Check out their examples page for ideas: https://carbonmade.com/examples

Behance. Another all-purpose portfolio option.
https://www.behance.net

Squarespace. Squarespace has a robust site builder that affords a high level of customization.
https://www.squarespace.com

WordPress.com. WordPress has a huge pool of free and paid plugins to customize your page how you see fit.
https://wordpress.com

Vimeo. If you'll be hosting reels or video (to show off animation, sound design, cinematics, etc), Vimeo has some of the highest quality video hosting around.
https://vimeo.com
If you end up using WordPress, the Vimeography plugin will make showcasing them even easier: https://vimeography.com

For Programmers

GitHub. If you aren't using it already, set up a GitHub account and use it to show off your programming projects.
https://github.com

For Audio Designers

SoundCloud. SoundCloud is tailor-made for sharing songs and audio.
https://soundcloud.com

For Artists

dribbble.com. Dribbble is laser-focused on visual designers, so making your home here makes sense.

https://dribbble.com

Reference Material [Reading]
This article has a comparison of some general-purpose website builder options:
http://www.websitebuilderexpert.com/wix-vs-weebly-vs-squarespace-vs-jimdo

The key rule to remember is this: **Only showcase your best work**.

Don't show everything you've done since middle school - only highlight your best work.

If you create a highlight reel, cap it at two minutes at the absolute maximum and only include your best work.

"I hadn't released any projects when I was hired [at DreamSail], so I had to rely on my own personal experiments and demos. So since I didn't have the strongest body of work, I had to present it well and prove that, even with no releases, I knew what I was doing."
  —Neil Sveri
  Programmer and Co-Founder | DreamSail Games

Make sure the first thing people see in your portfolio is succinct, easy to access and doesn't include too much description text on the screen. Get right to the content.

To people being introduced to you through your site, your portfolio is your first impression. Make an excellent one.

- **Artists:** Only show your best illustrations, concept art, renders, animations, etc.
- **Programmers**: Only show your best tech demos, sample code, technical blogs, etc.
- **Designers:** Only show your best design docs, paper prototypes, animatics, etc.
- **Audio Designers**: Only show your best work, either as sound replacement videos or game captures of original works.

- **Producers**: Only show your best postmortems, project summaries, pitches, etc.
- **Writers**: Only show your best treatments, spec scripts, dialog samples, sample fiction, etc.

Industry Talk
- *Sound Replacement Video*: This isn't generally used in the industry, but in this context it refers to a video of gameplay footage where all the sounds have been replaced. Sound designers use these to showcase their sound design and mixing skills.
- *Game Capture*: Gameplay footage recorded from actual gameplay.
- *Postmortem*: A report about something that happened after the fact. In game development, these usually refer to reports about how a game's development process went after it has finished, usually so the team can learn from their mistakes and improve.

Here are some good examples of portfolio sites:

Game Design
Magnar Jenssen
http://magnarj.net

Jack Lewis
www.jacklewisgamedesigner.com

David Wallin
http://www.davidwallin.net

Steve Massey
http://madmassey.com

Nicolas Bombray
http://www.nicolasbombray.com

Art
Morteza Ramezanali
www.cgdna.com/live

Paul Pepera
www.peperaart.com

John Gaertner
http://www.scribblepunk.com

Programming
Molly Jameson
http://www.mollyjameson.com

Daniel Soltyka
www.danielsoltyka.com

Dan Wellman
http://www.danwellman.com

Audio
Andrew Shcherbak
http://www.pencilboxsounds.com

Jordan Fehr
http://www.jordanfehr.com

Danny Armstrong
http://www.dannyarmstrongaudio.com

Production
Benjamin Roye
www.benroye.com

Carmela DeNero
http://cdenero.weebly.com/portfolio.html

Dante Medina
www.dantemedina.net

Writing
Leanne C. Taylor-Giles
http://www.leannectaylor.com

David J. Tiegen
http://davidjtiegen.com

Alex Kain
http://www.alexkain.net

4. Learn grammar and spelling

If there are spelling errors in your cover letter, that's a strike against you. If there are grammatical errors in your resume or portfolio materials, that's a strike against you. Poor grammar and spelling loudly communicate that you don't pay attention to details. When trying to break into games, you want all the advantages you can have.

Written communication is a critical part of the game development process. Being able to write and communicate well is foundational to any specialized work you may be doing. If your grammar or spelling needs work, fix it.

This also applies to spoken communication. Being clear and understandable will make a world of difference in working with others. Make an effort to use your sentences carefully. If someone seems like they don't understand what you're asking or explaining, ask them if it makes sense. Taking the time to make sure you are understood will save lots of time later when issues come up due to miscommunication.

English may not be your first language. In that case, spend the extra time to learn proper grammar and spelling, and ask a friend with native language proficiency to look over your portfolio materials/website/etc. The honest truth is that hiring managers won't be sympathetic to your challenges - they're just looking to mitigate risk with their next hire, and someone who literally can't speak the language poses more of a risk than someone who can. The people who make hiring decisions at game companies are extremely busy people, so if they review a resume riddled with typos, you better believe it's going right in the trash.

Of course, this applies to English grammar and spelling when applying for jobs at English-speaking game companies. Wherever you're planning to work and live, identify the primary language that the studio uses and improve your skills as much as possible.

Step 4: Make Contacts

"When you're first getting started, the #1 most important thing you can do is attend events for your local games community, talk to people about the projects they're working on, and keep an ear to the ground for opportunities for which you might be eligible."
       —*Caitlin L. Conner*
       Lead Narrative Designer | Gameloft

You need people. If you're going to move up from Unknown to Industry Hopeful to Professional Game Developer, you're going to need help.

You need other people during your journey to push you to evolve, clue you in about opportunities and keep you motivated when things seem impossible. Breaking into games is difficult to do and you can't do it in a vacuum.

Why Do I Need People?

Having a solid network in the games industry is the most efficient and time-honored way to break in. Because the games industry is a surprisingly small world, you never know where people you meet will end up.

Here's why having a robust network is key to breaking into games.

1. The Network Effect

Meeting other industry hopefuls is an incredibly valuable use of your time. These peers of yours might partner with you on portfolio projects, introduce you to important people you otherwise wouldn't have access to and provide crucial feedback on your projects as you improve your development skills.

If you're wary of becoming too friendly with other industry hopefuls because they might compete with you for jobs, you can stop thinking that right now. To the short-sighted, yes, your fellow industry hopefuls are competing with you for the same pool of entry-level jobs. However, in the long view they are actually your support system.

Should one of your industry hopeful friends get hired instead of you at a well-known game company, that doesn't mean they've stolen an opportunity from you. In reality, it means you now have a highly valuable contact on the inside. And the next time they have another entry level position open, you'll be the first to know.

Shine Theory
For more insight on why your fellow industry hopefuls are your peers and not your competition, read about Ann Friedman's concept of Shine Theory. The idea is that instead of women being overly competitive, they can work together to make each other shine brighter.
http://nymag.com/thecut/2013/05/shine-theory-how-to-stop-female-competition.html

2. Establish Your Reputation

By meeting other industry hopefuls and game devs and displaying your competence and ever-evolving skills, you're increasing the likelihood of one of them wanting to work with you one day.

Remember that the more people you come into contact and connect with, the higher the odds are that some of them will eventually climb to the upper levels in established game companies. Should that happen, you'll want them to think of you as that extremely competent person they should pull in as soon as they can clear it with HR.

3. Practice Collaborating

Modern game development is an intensely collaborative process. By meeting and working on projects with other people, you'll get invaluable practice building consensus with others, compromising on tasks, planning ahead with multiple stakeholders, and working in a team. The more experience you get at this, the better equipped you'll be to work in a team setting when you find yourself at a studio.

Industry Talk
- *Stakeholder*: Someone who has something at stake in the work being done. If you are working on a game that is being published and funded by a publisher, then the publisher is a stakeholder in your project.

"Make games with others as soon as you can, as it's the only way you'll really start to learn what's involved and why it's important to rein in project scope and everyone's expectations."
  —Evan Skolnick
  Senior Writer | Telltale Games

4. The Insider

The number one way to get a job at a game company is to have a personal contact on the inside. The games industry is surprisingly small and personal connections carry a lot of weight, especially if someone the hiring manager trusts is vouching for you.

However, if you're just starting out on your game industry journey, you're not likely to strike up meaningful relationships with game developers out of nowhere. Fortunately there are many other benefits to making contacts as you evolve your skills and develop an understanding of how the games business works.

5. Your Support System

When you hit lulls in your game industry career - whether it's layoffs, studio closures, canceled projects, other life events - your network will become your professional support system. If you've taken the care to cultivate a solid, functioning network, you might be surprised how much support comes bursting out of it when you need it the most.

But just like planning for a rainy day, you have to plan ahead in order to be covered. With a well-kept network, you'll have a much better shot at getting back on your feet faster.

Where Do I Meet People?

You can make contacts online or remotely, but making meaningful connections is best done in-person.

Here are some good places to start:

1. IGDA meetings

The IGDA (International Game Developers Association) is the game industry's largest non-profit professional association, with chapters in major cities all around the world. Find your closest active IGDA chapter, go to the meetings and meet everyone. Offering to help out with organizing events is an excellent way to introduce yourself and display your competence.

If the closest chapter is two hours away and only holds events every two months, find a way to get to every one. If there's no active chapter near you, start one.

2. Game development meetups

Look for meetups on meetup.com relating to game development near you. Find out if the nearest colleges and universities have game development clubs. Look anywhere online for where game developers and aspiring developers make plans to meet and join them. These are the people who will help you reach your goal - and you can help them reach theirs.

3. Game jams

Game jams are an extremely fertile place to meet game development contacts. These events generally last for a weekend. People show up at a host site, usually a college or sponsoring tech company, form teams, are given a theme, and have 24-48 hours to complete a small game using the assigned theme.

The largest, the Global Game Jam, takes place every January, with sites all around the world. Cities with active game development communities will often hold smaller game jams all year long.

Game jams are excellent for several reasons:

1. They're an ideal place to meet like-minded people interested in game development.
2. They let you get a glimpse at other people's work ethic and skills as you work alongside them to complete tasks under pressure.
3. They're excellent for bonding with new friends in a condensed time period due to the artificial time pressure.
4. At the end of the jam, you'll have a finished (or almost finished) game for your portfolio.
5. Finally, they're fun as hell!

You will learn a lot at game jams and you'll have a good time doing it. What's not to like?

But I Live in the Boonies!

If none of the above types of events happen even remotely close to you, you still have options.

Form a local game development club. Partner with a university to donate space and advertise the next meeting. Find people near you in online game development forums. You may have to get creative here, and that's OK.

If you live on a deserted island in the middle of the ocean and there's literally nobody around for hundreds of miles, you can still meet people online. Engage other hopefuls on game development forums and Twitter. Instead of game jams, enter online game jam events like Ludum Dare. Find like-minded developers on the TIGSource forums. Comb through the best games and talk to the developers through Twitter.

Above all, be prepared to move at some point in your journey. People who already live near studios have an advantage, and others hungrier to break in will make a point to move closer to studio hubs for this same reason. Sooner or later, you will have to get to where the jobs are.

"I learned that taking chances was the only way I was going to learn and evolve as a person and a developer."
　—Nick Madonna
　Founder/Business Development | PHL Collective

Highly Recommended Reading: Effective Networking in the Game Industry

Darius Kazemi's article series Effective Networking in the Game Industry is an exceptional resource for learning the ins and outs of getting to know game developers. Read all of these articles.

Darius has since changed his site and moved on from the games industry, but luckily an archived version is still available thanks to archive.org: https://web.archive.org/web/20110126093153/http://tinysubversions.com/effective-networking

A Note For the Introverted

"I overcame my personal awkwardness to become competent at meeting people at game industry functions, i.e. networking. This is a critical skill and not something that came naturally. I just put myself out there and eventually got better at it over time."
　—Josh Raab
　Associate Game Designer | Big Huge Games

If the thought of walking into a room full of strangers scares the hell out of you, you're in for an important lesson in willpower and personal growth.

Yes, it will be scary. Yes, you will be awkward at first. But over time, as you start to understand how critical your mission to break into the games industry is to you, your unnecessary fear of social settings will melt away. You get to talk about videogames with these people, for goodness sake! Plus, since the game industry has a tendency to attract the introverted, you can rest assured that most of the people you'll meet are feeling the same thing as you.

Soon, you'll feel less anxious about in-person meetings, and will start to actually look forward to them. After enough time you'll have trouble remembering when you were nervous at all.

If you're nervous about having to become more outgoing in order to break into games, relax. It will take time, but the truth is this process will help you become a more well-rounded human being - with the added benefit of a career in games to boot.

Don't Accept Defeat. No matter how hard it may seem to meet people, you must not give up. Getting into games is a group effort and you will need at least a few peers to help propel you to your goal. Be creative. Find avenues to network that work for your situation. You know you can do this.

You're Not Alone. The game industry is well-known for attracting introverts and people with introvert sensibilities. There's a good chance that other people you meet will feel the same way you do, and that should help take some of the pressure off.

Fool-Proof Conversation Starters. At a loss for how to talk to people at a game development event? Use any of these icebreakers to get things going:

- *What are you playing these days?*
- *What part of game development do you do?*
- *What are you working on now?*
- *Have you played [newly-released game that you have played]?*

Remember, you may have only just met this person, but your shared love of games is already something you have in common.

Advanced Networking Move: Become the Press

Start a game industry-related blog. Get good at writing. Once you have some pieces you would be proud to show strangers, reach out to local (and non-local) game developers who make games you like, asking to interview them for a post about their game industry experience or current projects. Include some samples of your past articles to prove that you can put together an article worthy of their time.

When you publish the piece, you'll not only have made a good contact, but they'll most likely share it on social media and introduce you to a new audience.

If you continue writing quality posts at a regular frequency, you can also try applying for press passes at game and game-related conferences in exchange for coverage. A press pass can be a great way to get introduced to people and opportunities you wouldn't be exposed to otherwise.

Here's a good resource for finding game-related events:

Reference Material [Tool]
GameConfs
http://www.gameconfs.com

Again, this will work only if you are a good writer. You'll also need to follow through with your obligation as press - meaning, if you promise to cover an event or interview someone for a blog post, you'd better actually write the blog post. Taking advantage of your position as press is a surefire way to earn a reputation as a shill to be avoided. Consider this advanced tactic with caution.

Step 5: Get Involved

Going to game industry events and meeting people is excellent, but you can go a step further. Getting involved with the game dev community gives you avenues to showcase your value as a future collaborator/employee, and gives you a chance to identify people and companies you'd want to work with.

Here are some ways to get involved.

Write for Game Sites

Find a game news site that's looking for writers and apply to write for them. If the site pays very little or nothing at all, then you have a decision to make.

If you are being supported by family or a spouse and you aren't financially responsible for yourself or a household, working for a low or no-paying site like this can serve as an interesting hobby that can help teach you more about your industry as well as give yourself a better way to introduce yourself at events. Remember that since you aren't being fairly compensated, you should not have any obligation to treat this activity like a full-time job - so if other job opportunities come along, or you find yourself unable to keep working, you are totally in the right to stop writing for them.

As a matter of fact, one of the first things I did to break into the industry was write for a bottom-rung game news site. Not only did they not pay anyone, but if we had to write a review, we had to buy the game ourselves! The conditions were ridiculous, but writing for them allowed me to go to E3 and GDC as a member of the press and meet key contacts that helped me eventually break in.

Industry Talk
- *E3*: The Electronic Entertainment Expo. E3 is a huge annual videogame trade show that usually happens in LA in the summer.

They Broke In as Press

There's a good precedent for writers in the games press making the jump to development. Here are a few notable examples you can research:

Greg Kasavin

Kasavin started as a writer for Gamespot, eventually working his way up to Editor in Chief before leaving to work for EA as an producer. He's most well-known for cofounding Supergiant, creator of *Bastion* and *Transistor*.

Rhianna Pratchett

Pratchett wrote for PC Zone and covered games for The Guardian before branching out into game writing for *Overlord*, *Tomb Raider*, *Mirror's Edge*, *Heavenly Sword*, and more.

Tom Francis

Francis taught himself enough programming while working at PC Gamer UK to develop the indie hit *Gunpoint*, leveraging his industry connections to help bring about a successful launch.

Anthony Burch

Burch is well-known for his webseries "Hey Ash, Whatcha Playin'?" but he also wrote reviews for Destructoid before getting hired as a writer at Gearbox, Telltale and Riot.

Erik Wolpaw and Chet Faliszek

Wolpaw and Faliszek are revered creative forces at Valve, but before they made their mark with *Team Fortress* 2 and *Portal*, they co-wrote the infamous gaming blog Old Man Murray.

Jamil Moledina

Moledina was the Editor in Chief of industry publication Game Developer Magazine before moving on to run the Game Developers Conference. After that came time at EA, a few mobile game startups, and Google.

Volunteer at Conventions

The Game Developers Conference (GDC) in San Francisco, IndieCade in California and New York, the Penny Arcade Expo (PAX) conventions - they all have volunteer programs that you can join.

In exchange for your time helping run the show, you'll have unprecedented access to what goes on behind the scenes, and will be easily able to meet a variety of developers. Plus, you'll be volunteering alongside fellow hopefuls who will one day become game developers. Volunteering at events is an incredibly productive use of your time as an industry hopeful.

Be Helpful to Others

Not everything you do has to be focused around you. There's an incredible advantage to be gained by purposefully helping others you encounter in your path to the game industry.

It connects you. Once people understand that you're a helpful resource, they're more likely to come to you when they encounter job openings or other opportunities in the hopes that you can put them in touch with someone suitable. This way, you'll be one of the first to know when someone comes across a freelance job they don't have time for or a full-time position that just opened up.

It costs nothing. Connecting people to your contacts or opportunities that they're looking for, offering constructive feedback when appropriate, or simply helping get the word out about their project if it's something you endorse can mean a lot to someone - and it doesn't cost you anything. Helping other people in a meaningful way earns you goodwill and a reputation as someone who is useful and intelligent. This is exactly how you want to present yourself to your network.

It comes back around. The more you help people along your journey to game development, the more you'll find those people have a tendency of coming back to help you out when you need it most. In the world of professional networking, karma is most definitely a real thing.

Ways that you can be helpful include:

1. Connecting people to opportunities

This goes beyond jobs. Say your friend Marguerite is working on an indie game for one of the new VR platforms, and she's stuck on a technical problem. As it happens, you know that Nate, another developer in your game development circles, is working on a similar game at a local game studio for the same VR platform.

"Being proactive at the right time and in the right way makes all the difference when turning an interest into a career."
  —*Evan Berman*
  Senior Community Manager | Bethesda Softworks

Taking the time to connect them to each other provides Marguerite with value - a peer encountering similar obstacles - and provides Nate with an additional sounding board for his own projects. Plus, if a job for a VR developer ever opens up at Nate's company and he ends up hiring your friend based on the connection you made, both of them will be grateful and will hold you in higher esteem.

Being known as a person who creates opportunities is an excellent thing to be for an industry hopeful.

2. Giving critiques (if asked)

Game development is an iterative process, and getting feedback from playtesters is critical to producing a great experience. If someone asks if you could play their game and give feedback, do it! What costs you a few minutes of time to play their demo and put together some thoughts is incredibly valuable for their development process.

Industry Talk
- *Iterative*: Something that is repeated. The core idea is that nobody knows what makes a fun game, so when you start working on something, you'll need to make many changes to the idea in practice until it becomes something good.

Offering to test the games of people you meet at networking events is good, but a better way to go about this is to attend events focused on gathering playtester feedback. For example, during the school year NYU hosts Playtest Thursdays, a weekly event where students solicit feedback for games in progress. If there aren't any playtest-focused events near you, organize some.

Reference Material [Link]
NYU's Playtest Thursdays:
http://gamecenter.nyu.edu/events/playtest-thursdays

Gearbox's Raison Varner on Giving Good Feedback
"When giving feedback on games, talk about experiences, not opinions. Always try to frame your opinions as reactions to things instead of preferential statements like 'I don't like shooters' or 'I hate the loot system.'

Rather express those thoughts as:

'I usually don't play shooters, but what I liked about your game was…'
'I usually don't play shooters, so bear that in mind when I say…'
'I experienced frustration with the loot system because…'

This keeps conversation in more of a mechanical or logic driven process. If opinions are being given without detailed information, it becomes an emotional conversation instead and that is the immediate death of critique."

> —*Raison Varner*
> *Sound Designer and Composer | Gearbox Software*

3. Giving careful critiques (if not asked)

Game development can be an intensely personal process. If someone shows you their game but doesn't seem to be able to handle criticism, you can first ask if they want to hear your thoughts. If they do, and you're still not sure they can handle constructive, honest feedback, make sure to present your thoughts in a compassionate way.

Don't sugarcoat your feedback - telling somebody they're on the right track when their demo is a mess isn't doing them any favors. Rather, frame your comments in a constructive way, telling them things they're doing right that can be made even better with some changes.

Remember that your fellow industry hopefuls may not have any professional experience yet, and may not be able to process feedback objectively. This is especially true if you just met them or don't know them very well.

Before you start giving feedback, make sure you first learn how to give constructive criticism. Giving people a laundry list of everything you hate about their project is not how to do it. Unanimous praise is equally unhelpful - constructive criticism is what you're after.

Explain why you think something doesn't work in objective terms, talk about your specific reaction and decision process in coming to that conclusion, and offer some possible ways to make it better. Giving feedback from an empathetic place is much more helpful for the creator.

Here are some resources in learning how to give and ask for better game feedback:

Reference Material [Reading]
A Simple Way to Get Great Playtesting Feedback
http://www.wiltgren.com/2016/01/18/a-simple-way-to-get-great-playtesting-feedback

Extra Credits - Playtesting - How to Get Good Feedback on Your Game
https://www.youtube.com/watch?v=on7endO4lPY

4. Promote projects that speak to you

If someone you meet in your local industry scene is working on a project that resonates with you in some way, help promote it! This can be anything from a simple Facebook or Twitter mention to writing about their game on your blog to helping them run a booth at a playtest event or game expo.

Don't look to be rewarded for your enthusiasm - do it because you generally like the game and the developer. Not only will the developer appreciate everything you've done to support them, but you might meet other people interested in the game that you can connect with through your common thread. Positivity breeds opportunity.

Give Wholehearted Endorsements
If you choose to promote projects on social media, try to write an original post in your own words that expresses your enthusiasm and communicates why your followers should care about the project.

While retweeting or reposting the original post is still helpful if that's all you can do, an original post in your own words is vastly more valuable to your followers and the project you're trying to promote.

Original remarks from you will be more interesting for your followers, and the creator will be more appreciative. Put thought into this.

5. Giving gifts of time and expertise

As you work at getting into games, you might find other industry hopefuls asking you questions, asking for introductions, or seeking advice about how to move forward. Giving gifts of your time and expertise so far - either by replying to their emails with well-thought-out answers, making an introduction if it seems appropriate to you, or even agreeing to meet for coffee - is a great way to use your time to help others.

Step 6: Display Your Competency and Value

"Practice your skills and make connections. You need both skills and connections to have a shot."
　—*Josh Raab*
　Associate Game Designer | Big Huge Games

When someone you know comes across a job opportunity that's a fit for you, you want them to do two things:

1. **Think of you for the job**
2. **Be confident you can do it well**

The best way to have them think this is to display your competency and value so you **mitigate the risk** in their minds of your not being able to do the job.

This is why you do all of the things mentioned in this chapter.

This is why you:

- **Make** games/prototypes and bring them to playtest events, solicit feedback from people and playtesters, and continuously improve them;
- **Help** people in your game dev community by providing feedback, helping organize events, and connecting people to opportunities;
- **Write** blogs, articles, etc, to show your level of insight and involvement in game development.

Make, Help, Write. Doing as many of these activities as possible as well as you can will demonstrate your competency and value to potential collaborators.

Who Am I Impressing?

As you do these things, you're not trying to impress anyone in particular. You're trying to impress **everybody**.

The reality of breaking into games is you can never predict how it'll happen. That super geeky amateur programmer who brought his homemade 2D engine to the show-and-tell event last month? Now he's the lead physics programmer for a Triple-A title. The high school student who had a thousand questions about how you use Photoshop? She just got into DigiPen, and will be learning how to make games every day for the next four years.

Industry Talk
- *Triple-A*: A term used to refer to the top-tier category of games in terms of budget and production value.
- *DigiPen*: A college in Seattle that focuses on game development as a career.

You never know where people will go in this business. Be friendly to everyone. Demonstrate your competency and value everywhere you go. Help people if you can do something for them. Don't just think of yourself - you're all in this together.

Step 7: Unify Your Messaging

Having a LinkedIn, Twitter and portfolio website are all important. But do all of your professional online identities make sense? Do you present yourself as a level designer on LinkedIn, but a game designer on your portfolio? Do you have a business card? Does your business card look professional? Does the design match your portfolio site?

The more effectively you unify your messaging, the easier you'll make it for people who might potentially want to hire you. If you want to get a job as a producer, and you have some experience working as a tester last summer, but what you **really** want to do is be a game designer, don't brand yourself as all three of those. Present yourself with as unified an identity as possible.

Case Study: Business Card

When I was looking for work as a game designer and writer, I wanted a business card design that communicated exactly what I was about. With the Game Developers Conference coming up, I wanted something special that would stand out to people I gave them to.

I ended up settling on two card designs: one for networking during the day, and another for the parties at night:

Daytime card design:

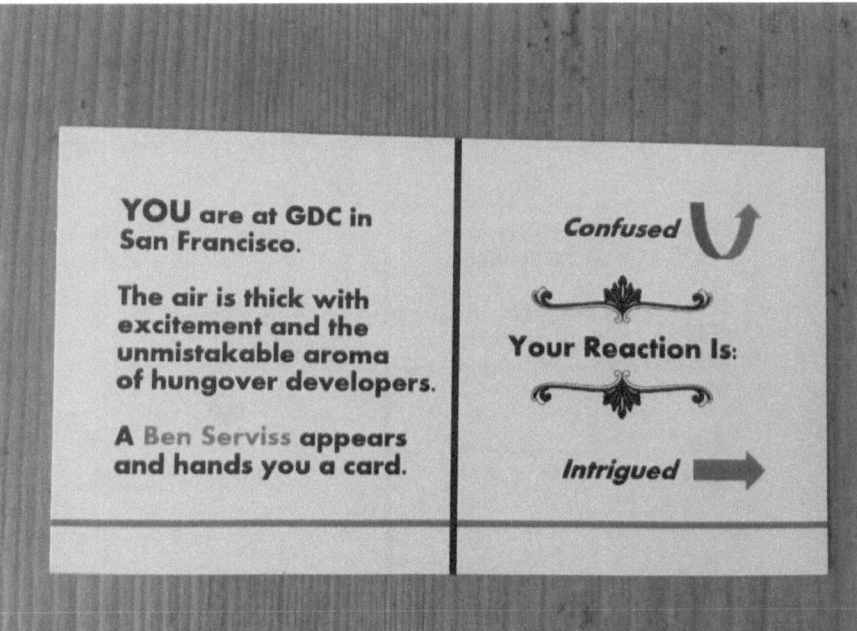

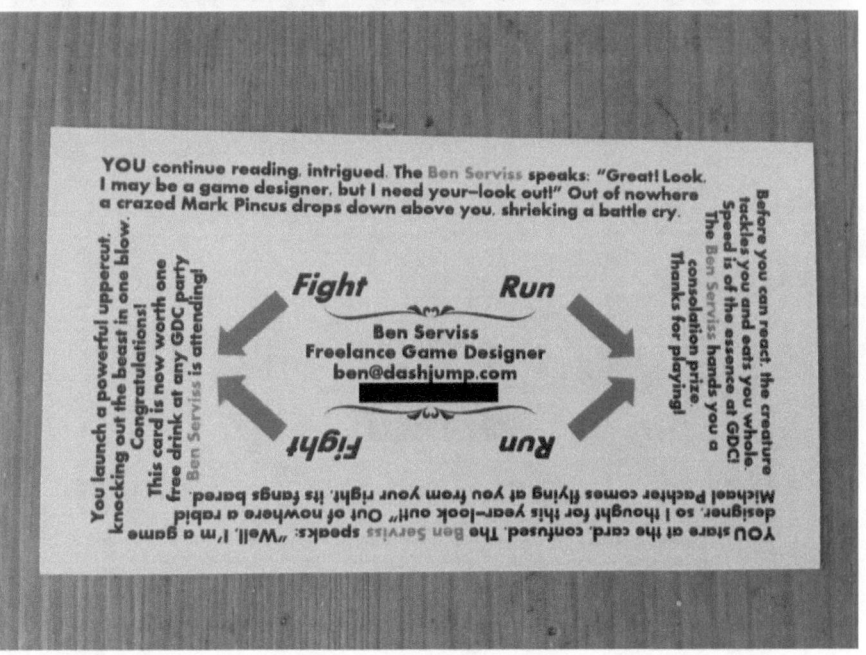

Nighttime card design:

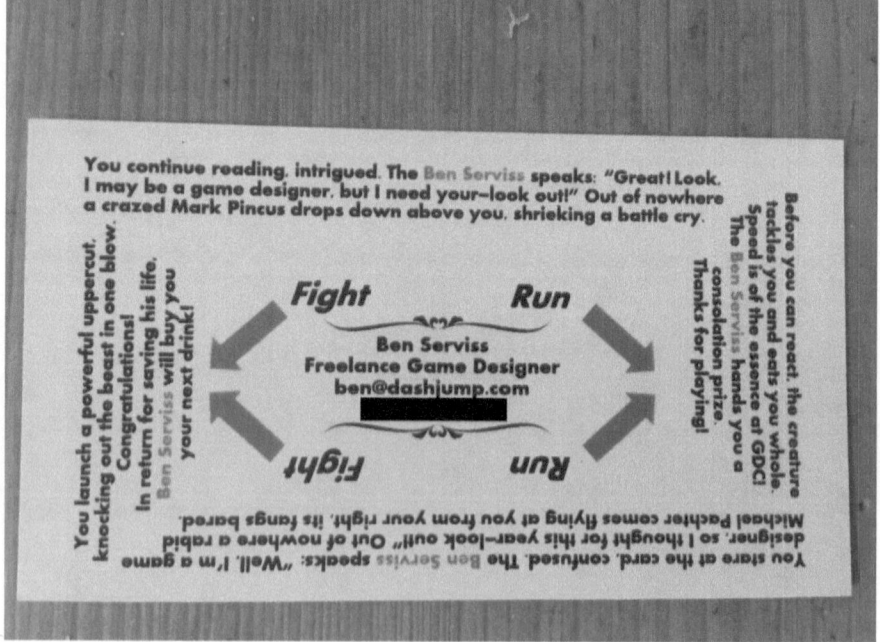

As soon as I handed people this card, it was clear that I was all about the narrative end of game design.

Fun fact: I gave one of these to one of the co-founders of text-based game company Choice of Games at that conference, which led to writing my text game *The Last Monster Master* for them. My previous experience and writing samples helped seal the deal, but that card was the perfect introduction.

After the conference, I solicited some feedback on the cards' design. The overall feedback was that the idea was good in concept, but the print was too small. For the next batch, I revised them to reduce complexity while still retaining the spirit of what I was trying to say.

Revised card design:

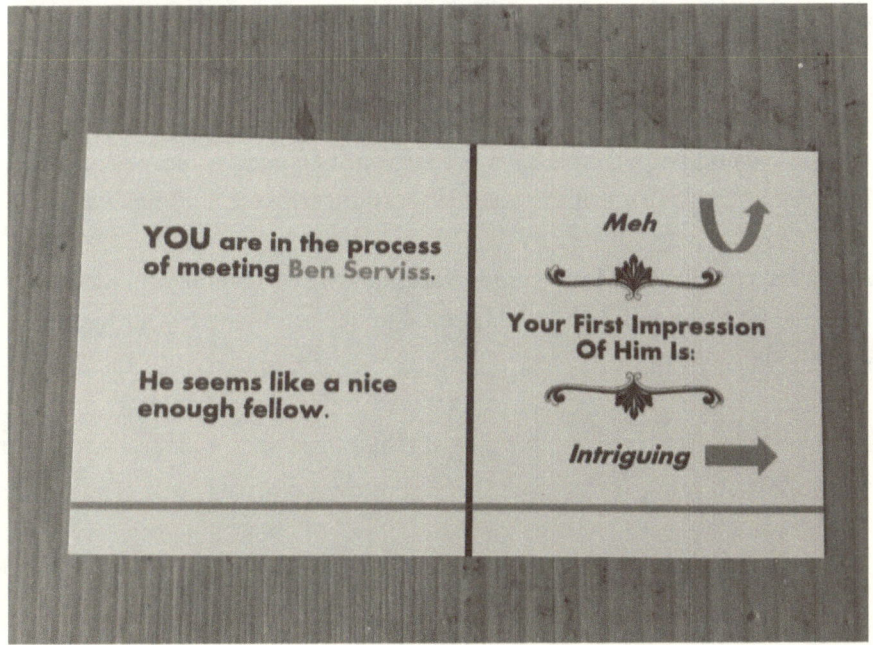

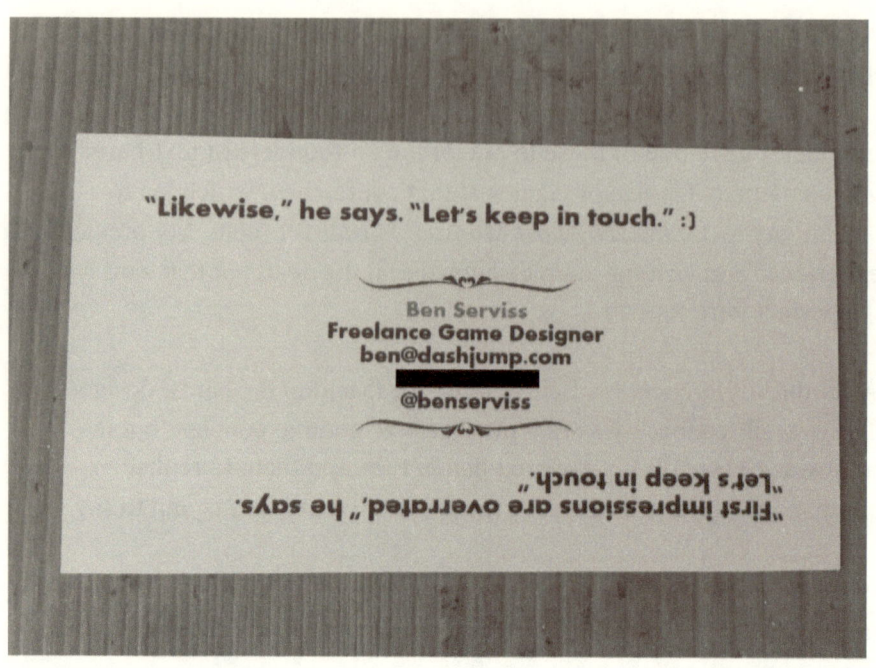

Not only was this version much easier to read, but the feedback from the first version helped create a more streamlined general-purpose card that I could use the rest of the year. Hooray for iteration and feedback!

Whatever you want to do in games, finding a way to brand yourself as that specific thing will help other people understand where your talents and inclinations lie.

Step 8: Apply, Apply, Apply

"I applied to every single storytelling job that I could find in game development. Each application also required I complete a writing test, so that expanded my portfolio while also giving me practice at writing to a deadline."
 —*John McLean-Foreman*
 Narrative Director/Lead Writer | Freelance

Now that you have projects to share, an online presence to vouch for you, a network to bounce ideas off of and a sound idea of how the game industry works, it's time to apply for jobs.

Part of the work here will simply be finding entry-level jobs for your chosen field. Because many positions are filled via personal contacts and through networks of people who already work at the company, a large amount of game jobs are never advertised. However, it does happen, and one of the most challenging parts of applying is just finding positions to apply to in the first place.

Remember that you'll want to aim for entry-level positions to start with. While it may seem like you don't have anything to lose applying for jobs that require at least three years of experience and a credit on shipped Triple-A games, you'd be better off spending that time improving your skills.

Here are some resources to keep in mind as you search for job openings:

Reference Material [Tools]
Gamasutra Job Board
http://jobs.gamasutra.com

IGDA Job Board
http://careers.igda.org
Note: It's always a good idea to go directly to the job sites for specific studios where you want to work. Usually, they'll be the first to have new job openings.

GameDevMap
https://www.gamedevmap.com
Note: The map may be slightly outdated depending on the city, but it can still be a useful resource.

Remember as you apply for jobs that the most common way to find a job in games is through a personal connection to someone who works at the studio you're applying to. Having a contact at the studio who can make sure your resume and portfolio get in front of a decision maker instead of thrown in the trash is an enormous advantage.

You can certainly send in blind applications to companies if you don't have any contacts there, but know that the odds of receiving a positive response (or even a response at all) is significantly lower.

Bonus Step 9: Become an Organizer

Are there local game dev meetups near you? If you go to any, do you know who the organizer is? There's a chance you do, and that reason alone is why it's a good idea to become one.

Organizing events is an excellent way to get acquainted with your local game dev scene quickly. By necessity, you'll need to meet people who can provide space for events, companies who may want to sponsor events, and all the local game developers and industry hopefuls.

Organizing events, even relatively unstructured ones like a social meetup at a bar, positions you as a person of note in the community who is good at making things happen. It'll help make you an advocate for your local game dev community and is a very effective way to multiply your game dev network.

Bonus Step 10: Learn From the Past

While it's hard to break into games, fortunately for you there are plenty of people who have already done it. If you look hard enough, you can find their stories in plain sight.

Find as many of these as you can. Find interviews with well-known and unknown developers about how they found their start. Read up on what they did to prepare themselves for the industry, how they made connections, and how they struck when the opportunity presented itself.

While you shouldn't expect to copy anyone's breaking-in story, especially if they did so a decade ago or more when things were different, pay attention to the common themes running through all these stories. Let them guide you as you figure this out.

Another way to do this is to start with companies you're interested in working at. Google around for interviews, PR pieces or "meet the team"-style blog posts. Some companies even write posts specifying what they look for in a candidate - definitely follow their advice!

The last thing you can do is critical: When you meet game developers at events, ask them how they got their start. You may want to save this for a follow-up question after you meet them, since nobody wants to feel like they're being grilled. However, an email follow-up after initially meeting them asking for their story is a reasonable request.

Here are some notable breaking-in stories to get you started:

Reference Material [Reading]
Todd Howard, Bethesda/ZeniMax
http://www.gameinformer.com/b/news/archive/2011/01/13/road-to-skyrim-the-todd-howard-interview.aspx

Tim Schafer, Double Fine
http://www.doublefine.com/news/comments/twenty_years_only_a_few_tears

Marius Fietzek, Double Fine
http://kotaku.com/5893454/genius-turns-job-application-into-lucasarts-adventure-game

Dave Voyales, Microsoft
http://www.davevoyles.com/how-did-i-get-started-in-evangelism-pt-1

Chris Bartlett, Epic
http://www.tk409.com/gettingajob.html

10 Killer Tips for Landing a Job with a AAA Game Developer (Advice from Naughty Dog)
https://www.gnomon.edu/blog/10-killer-tips-for-landing-a-job-with-a-aaa-game-developer

Breaking Into the Game Industry: Hi-Rez Studios video series
https://www.hirezstudios.com/breaking-in

Chapter 3: Rites of Passage

Walk the Path

"Growing as a person and growing as a developer are one and the same. The more you take in from life, the more knowledge you can apply to your craft."
—*Nick Madonna*
Founder/Business Development | PHL Collective

As you embark on the journey to the game industry, there are a few things you should make sure to do. These rites of passage will:

- Give you a better sense of the game industry, first from a local perspective, then a global one;
- Teach you immeasurable lessons about being a game developer; and
- Grant you fantastic networking opportunities to meet your fellow developers.

Local Meetups

Breaking into games starts on the local level. Find the biggest game development meetup near you and show up. It may be a regularly-scheduled IGDA meeting, a college-sponsored group, or a unique meetup specific to where you live. Don't be afraid to make an hour-long commute to get there - if that's what it takes, then that's what you have to do. In most cases, once you've gotten yourself there, most of the work is already done.

Once you're there, here's what you do.

Become a Regular

This part is actually easy! Make it a point to attend the best local meetups near you as much as you can. Before long, you'll start to recognize people, and people will start to recognize you. If talking to new people and making friends doesn't come naturally, the repetition of coming to meetup after meetup will make it easier to get to know everyone over time.

(Optional) Present Something

Some meetups are unstructured in nature. These might take the form of a scheduled hangout at a bar, a playtest night, a project showcase, or a game-playing event.

Other events may be centered on organized programming. These might include talks from game developers, student project presentations, panels about working in the industry, or a series of game idea pitches. If your local meetup does any programming-centered events, come up with a presentation that you think would be interesting to the other meetup members, and pitch your idea to the organizer.

Even if your meetup mostly does unstructured events, you can still always ask the organizer! If you have a good idea, take the initiative. Even if your idea is turned down this time, nobody will fault you for trying.

(Optional) Organize Something

If you can't think of something you would feel comfortable presenting, or if public speaking terrifies you, you can still help put something together behind the scenes.

Some ideas:

1. Organize a Break Into the Game Industry event

Ask local game developers if they'd like to talk about their experiences. If you can get a few people interested, put together a panel so they can discuss their individual paths. Another idea is to ask some of them to serve as guest judges for a student resume critique event to help students refine their resumes and portfolios.

2. Get a guest developer speaker

If you know a notable local game developer, or can get the attention of one who's in town, great! Ask if they'd like to talk about a game they just finished, or what it's like to work at their game studio, or the latest techniques in their discipline, or anything else they might want to discuss.

3. Get a guest faculty speaker

Find someone in the faculty at a local college's game development program and ask if they'd like to present. If you can get a few faculty members from different schools involved, have them do different talks on their respective programs.

4. Organize a game critique night

Pick a classic game, or a few of them, and ask people in your local game development scene to critique them in analytical ways. Is one game lauded for its addictive, yet simple gameplay? Pick it apart and identify what makes it so great. Does a recently-released game owe a great debt to a forgotten classic? Talk about the history behind the new game, looking at all the past titles that it built upon.

If you organize an event, you'll probably have the chance to offer brief opening remarks at the start of the meetup. Doing so is a great way to let everyone know that you helped put this event together, while still being able to enjoy it yourself.

A Note on Alcohol
Depending on the meetup, everyone might go to a bar afterward to hang out and socialize, or the entire meetup may just be a casual night at a bar. If the meetup is at a venue where alcohol is available, make sure to know your limits.

Drinking too much and acting inappropriately is exactly the opposite of how you want to behave in a networking situation, and is an extremely fast way to earn a bad reputation among your peers. When in doubt, have one drink and switch to non-alcoholic drinks for the rest of the meetup.

GGJ: Global Game Jam

"The goal of a game jam is to design a video game, either alone or in teams, as fast as is humanly possible; usually in a single weekend."
    -The Game Jam Survival Guide
        www.packtpub.com/game-development/game-jam-survival-guide

Why the GGJ?

Over the past decade or so, game jams have exploded from an industry-specific kind of event to fun bursts of creation open to all. While there is no current shortage of game jams in cities that are industry hubs, and there are more online-only game jams than ever before, the most important one to attend in your game development journey is the Global Game Jam.

A few things distinguish the GGJ from other game jams:

1. It's local…

To enter the GGJ, you have to either register at a GGJ-approved jam site, or create your own. This helps steer people toward larger hubs to attract the highest amount of people, which increases the pool of potential people you can meet and work with.

2. …and global.

The "Global" in GGJ isn't just for marketing purposes. Every year, people in countries around the world participate in the GGJ. By the time the jam ends, thousands of games will have been created.

3. It's well-organized.

Every year, the GGJ Executive Committee manages the schedule, the jam theme, the website that teams upload their games to, and the PR that accompanies the event. Taking some of the unknowns out of the process can help you focus on making games and meeting people.

4. It's respected.

At this point, most people in the industry know what the GGJ is. If you participate, it's at least a good talking point. If you end up with a finished game that you're proud of, then it's a nice portfolio addition.

5. It's a ton of fun.

Being a part of a game development-focused event on this scale is electrifying. Prepare to have a good time.

How Does it Work?

Here's roughly what you can expect at the Global Game Jam:

Day 1: Friday Evening

5:00 PM - 7:00 PM: Arrive at the site and check in
7:00 PM - 7:30 PM: Videos introducing the GGJ, explaining the rules and introducing the theme
7:30 PM - 8:30 PM: Form groups with other attendees
8:30 PM - 12:00 AM: Make a game!

Day 2: Saturday
All day: Make a game!

Day 3: Sunday
12:00 AM - 3:00 PM: Finish your game!
3:00 PM - 4:00 PM: On-site judges play all games, all participants can play the finished games
4:00 PM - 5:00 PM: Site-specific award presentations
5:00 PM - 7:00 PM: Hang out and play all the games

You take read more about the schedule at the GGJ site's FAQ page: http://globalgamejam.org/faq

So how can you get the most out of your GGJ experience?

Register at a Big Site

Finding the biggest GGJ site near you is the first step to meeting more like-minded people. Because you'll need people who can do a variety of tasks, including programming, art, sound and design, being around more people increases the chances that more specialists will be available.

To put it another way, if you go to a smaller site with only 15 people, three of whom are programmers, the teams without programmers will be at a disadvantage. Aim for the largest site you can reasonably get to over the weekend.

"Game jams were especially fantastic because they gave me incentive to work, had me meeting more experienced people, and would often result in me having a somewhat complete game at the end."
—*Neil Sveri*
Programmer and Co-Founder | DreamSail Games

Don't Worry

"Don't be frustrated by failure. Embrace it. LEARN from it. Constantly improve. Be happy with your work but never be content. Fail fast and happily move on to the next thing."
—*Coray Seifert*
Director of Production | Experiment 7

Even if it's your first game jam, there's no reason to feel intimidated. There is no way to lose or "screw up," even if you don't end up finishing your game. Game jams are meant to be fun because there is literally nothing at stake if your game isn't finished, isn't fun or doesn't work.

If that happens, learn from it! Try to find out what went wrong so you can do better next time. Remember that this experience, no matter how it turns out, will only help you improve.

Game Jam Tip: Halve the Scope
If you want to see improved results from your jam experience, try this: Whatever the scope you have in mind for your game, cut it in half. Things always take longer than you think, and it's far better to have a complete (or at least playable) short game than unplayable pieces of a much longer game.

Work With New People

While it can be tempting to work on something by yourself or default to working with people you already know, using the GGJ as an opportunity to branch out can be a key use of your time.

Working on stuff with people you just met is a huge part of why game jams are so effective in the first place:

1. It's the best working interview you can imagine.

Actually working with somebody - not reviewing their resume or portfolio, or relying on what they said they've done - is the single best way to size up someone's ability and skills.

Even if the people you're working with aren't in positions where they need to hire somebody right now, they might be in the future. And should that happen, wouldn't you want to be someone that comes to their mind as competent and valuable?

By working well with others and demonstrating your skills, aptitude and creativity, you'll send a powerful message that you're someone to consider for a job, should your game jam team members ever find themselves needing to hire someone.

No Really, It Works
This is exactly what happened to me at the 2014 Global Game Jam, but from the other end. I ended up working with a developer I had met at a meetup, and even though our game turned out to be hilariously janky, his work ethic and aptitude stayed with me, and I ended up referring him for some freelance design work when I got too busy.

2. You'll bond quickly.

The sustained burst of adrenaline that comes with doing the Global Game Jam means that you'll form powerful, vivid memories working with your new game dev buddies.

As long as you put in your best effort and cast a good impression, the experience will stick with you and your team members. This will help you later when suggesting future projects to work on together, or if one of them ever needs to hire someone.

3. It simulates game development in a highly compressed way.

The time constraints, push for creativity under pressure and rapid iteration process is a microcosm of the actual game development process. The more times you can get through the cycle of conceiving, prototyping, developing, testing and polishing a game, the more acquainted you'll get with the actual game development process.

Industry Talk
- *Polishing*: The process of taking something that is finished and good enough, and tweaking it so that it's as good as it can be. This refers to the literal act of polishing something to give it an extra sheen.

Over time, this will help improve the quality of your games, as well as prepare you for what to expect from a studio once you get your foot in the door.

Play the Games, Talk to Devs

When development time winds down on the last day, the jam site organizers usually ask all of the devs to submit their games and put them on display for the judges (and everyone else) to play.

You might be tempted to keep working on your game, put the finishing touches on your online submission, or take a long-overdue nap. Instead, take this time to play all the other games, and take note of ones you particularly like.

If your jam site gives out awards, stick around after and talk to the devs of the games you liked. Now's the time to nerd the hell out. Ask them about their development process, what tools they used, if they've done the GGJ before, if they're professional devs, what games they're playing, whatever else that's relevant. These are the people you probably want to be collaborating with and should know. Make an effort to follow up with them after - via Twitter, email, or whatever other channel makes the most sense.

(Bonus) Play Games Around the World

While the best relationships are formed in person, there's plenty of opportunities to connect with like-minded devs and aspiring devs online.

Because the GGJ's site doubles as a repository of games created all around the world during the jam, after it's all over take some time to play through games created at other sites. Look for "best games from GGJ" write-ups that curate some of the best games and play them.

Again, if you find any games that particularly resonate with you, reach out to the devs over whatever social media channel you can find them on. Explain what you like about their game, discuss the challenges you ran into on your project, ask about their process, etc.

The game development community is very comfortable with using the internet as a way to connect with people, so there's no reason why you can't make some promising contacts that way too. Don't let your physical location be a barrier.

GDC: The Game Developers Conference

"Your network in the industry can be everything. Attend the Game Developers Conference (GDC) in your area if at all possible, and do your best to make industry connections there. Trying to break into a game studio through the front door can be extremely challenging if you don't know anyone at all on the inside."
   —Evan Skolnick
   Senior Writer | Telltale Games

If there was ever a rite of passage to working in games, it's going to GDC. What started as a small gathering of developers in the 1980s has exploded into a week-long conference/summer camp/party/networking extravaganza that attracts over 25,000 game developers from all over the world.

I started going to GDC in 2005, and since then I've gone around eight times in all kinds of contexts. I've volunteered, covered it as press, gone as part of a studio, as a freelancer, and went without a pass at all. Later in this section I'll break down the benefits of each approach.

What To Expect

Over the past decade, GDC has settled on a more or less permanent home in San Francisco, and is held each year sometime in February or March. Here's a quick summary of what you can expect from a typical GDC schedule:

Sunday
- Arrive in San Francisco. Get a feel for the city and the convention center's layout.

Monday - Tuesday
- Day: Day-long tutorials focusing on specific areas of game design, like game design, animation, production, business, engineering and audio

- Night: Informal gatherings with people you meet, maybe a few sponsored parties

Wednesday - Friday
Day:
- Talks on every possible aspect of game development averaging at one hour in length
- The expo floor opens, with tons of vendors and opportunities to demo upcoming games and technologies
- The career fair opens, with many major and minor-league studios having some kind of presence
- The Independent Game Festival (IGF) Pavilion opens, allowing you to play the games up for IGF awards and meet their developers
- Lots of other special events and exhibits where you can play upcoming and experimental games, explore games history, and more

Night:
- The IGF Awards, which anoints the industry's next round of indie darlings (usually Wednesday night)
- The Game Developers Choice Awards, which crowns the industry's most critically-acclaimed games for the past year (usually Wednesday night right after the IGF Awards)
- An unbelievable amount of parties hosted by big-name studios (Microsoft, Sony, Valve, Blizzard), smaller developers (Wadget Eye), hardware manufacturers (AMD), media outlets (Destructoid, Pocket Gamer), software developers (Autodesk), service providers (Twitch) and more

Saturday
- Feel more exhausted than you've ever felt before in your entire life
- Drag yourself to a plane and pass out on the way home

The key takeaway: Your first GDC will blow your damn mind.

You will learn a ton from hearing industry veterans during the talks and tutorials. You'll meet other game developers, some already established, others trying to break in like yourself, from a wide range of backgrounds. You might even meet some of your game industry heroes.

The sheer amount of game industry energy will be exhilarating.

To maximize the benefit from your trip, and because a lot of the value that comes from GDC is in the networking, you'll want to make sure you're able to network to the best of your ability. Before you head out, practice networking at local events. Read the section about networking in this book, and follow the recommendations. GDC can be somewhat of an intimidating experience, so the more you can do to prepare, the better.

Next, I'll discuss the different ways you can attend and some of the hidden pros and cons to each approach.

Reference Materials [Reading]
Recommended reading for GDC prep:

Surviving GDC: Tips for Game Conference Success
http://gamedevelopment.tutsplus.com/articles/surviving-gdc-tips-for-game-conference-success--cms-20359

A Guide for First-Time Students at GDC
https://praliedutzel.wordpress.com/2012/03/01/a-guide-for-first-time-students-at-gdc

How To Make The Most Out Of Attending The Game Developers Conference (And Is It Worth It?)
https://www.nyfa.edu/student-resources/is-game-developers-conference-worth-it

Networking at GDC- A Beginner's Guide, Part 1
http://www.gamasutra.com/blogs/StephenFroeber/20140112/208457/Networking_at_GDC_A_Beginners_Guide_Part_1.php

Option One: Volunteer as a CA (Conference Associate)

As someone trying to break into games, one of the best things you can do is volunteer at GDC by being a CA. CAs help run the conference by managing lines for talks, helping speakers set up their presentations, and generally assisting with logistics for the conference.

In exchange for volunteering for a set number of hours during the week, you'll get a free all-access badge, access to the CA lounge, and a GIGANTIC ARMY OF INSTANT FRIENDS. I volunteered as a CA in 2014, and was astounded at both how large the network of CAs is throughout the industry and at how intensely close-knit everyone was.

Not only will you get the best introduction to what GDC is and how it works, but you'll also have the easiest time getting used to the lay of the land. It also helps that networking with other CAs is very painless.

In fact, the program is so beloved, that people keep returning to volunteer year after year - even after former industry hopefuls break in and have been working as professional developers for years.

Deadlines for CA applications may change year to year, so check back at the official GDC site for information: http://www.gdconf.com

Option Two: Get a Student Scholarship

If you're a student, this is an excellent option. While you won't have a ready-made community like the CA program, you'll be able to tap into a network of fellow scholarship winners.

For a long time, the sole option for student scholarships was the IGDA Foundation Student Scholarship, sponsored by the IGDA Foundation. If accepted, you'd receive an all-access pass and be paired with an industry mentor to help you navigate GDC. While the free pass is great, access to a mentor can be a critical boost in getting introductions to people who can open up doors.

Now, the IGDA scholarship is just one option among many. When the GDC site gets updated for the next upcoming conference, take a look at the scholarships being offered and apply for all of the ones that apply to you.

Check the official GDC site for scholarships here:
http://www.gdconf.com/attend/scholarships.html

Option Three: Win a Contest

Going beyond the scholarships available through GDC, scout around for new opportunities that may not be officially partnered with the conference. In the past, Microsoft has run a "Game Changer" contest for female computer science students, which included a free all-access GDC pass and exclusive networking opportunities as prizes.

More info here:
http://blogs.microsoft.com/jobs/international/are-you-a-game-changer

You can also check to see if any local institutions like colleges or meetups offer free or subsidized passes to GDC. For example, in years past the game development community Playcrafting ran a contest for a free GDC pass. Entering these kinds of contests is usually free, so you don't have much to lose.

The winner from 2014:
http://www.meetup.com/gaming/messages/66171142

Yet another option is the GDC Lottery for Low Income Attendees. If you win, you'll get an Expo Pass (which doesn't include access to sessions or classes) at no charge.
http://www.gdconf.com/low-income-pass-lottery

Option Four: Buy a Pass

If all else fails, you can always buy a pass. You have several options here depending on your specific goals, interests and available budget:

Note: Pass options and prices here are from the 2016 GDC. Specific pass options and prices are subject to change year to year.

Pass	Price	Description
All Access Pass	$1,599 - $2,099	Everything from Monday - Friday. Good if you want to go to as many sessions as possible and soak everything up and can afford it.
Main Conference Pass	$999 - $1,699	Everything from Wednesday - Friday. Good if you want to focus on the shorter talks, or if you're not arriving until Wednesday.
Summits, Tutorials & Bootcamps Pass	$799 - $999	Everything from Monday - Tuesday. Good if you want to focus on the longer day-long tutorials and deep dives into subject matter and if you want to focus on networking later in the week.
Independent Game Summit Pass	$329	All IGS talks from Monday - Tuesday. Good if you want to learn about indie game development and want to focus on networking with indies devs.
Audio Track	$699 - $899	All audio-related talks. Good if you want to break in as a sound designer, composer, or any audio-related field and want to learn as much as you can.
Expo Pass	$199 - $249	Access to the Expo from Wednesday - Friday. Good if you're on a budget and want to focus on networking over learning about specific development practices.
Student Expo Pass	$79	Friday-only access to the Expo and limited programming. Not generally recommended, but can be better than nothing if you're a student on a tight budget.

Option Five: Skip the Pass (Veterans Only)

If all other options fail you, and you're dead-set on going to GDC this year, you can skip the pass altogether. Since the ultimate purpose of GDC as an industry hopeful is to grow your network, you can just as easily do this wandering the convention center halls. This approach relies more on your being proactive in striking up conversations and finding places to go, so make sure this sounds like something you'd be comfortable doing.

Also note that a lot of networking happens at night at the industry parties, so if you don't mind finagling your way inside, this could be a viable option.

In general, going without a pass is recommended for people who have been to GDC at least a couple of times so you have an idea of what to expect. If you're thinking about going without a pass for your first time, I would strongly reconsider taking the trip until you're able to go with one of the other options.

Optimize Networking for Results

"The goal is to be friendly, do not impose on others' time just to network, and be remembered as someone easy going, friendly and generally likable. Successful networking is just the result of making friends or becoming friendly acquaintances. It's not important that someone has your card, it's important that they remember their interaction as a pleasant experience."
    —Raison Varner
    Sound Designer and Composer | Gearbox Software

How do you know if you're networking right at GDC? It's very easy to find out:

If you can connect with people in a meaningful way after the conference, you're networking effectively.

The whole purpose of networking is to build a network that you can use to help reveal opportunities, while at the same time, you contribute value back to it. It's a virtuous circle that, when done with the right mindset, can propel you and your contacts to new career heights. For that to work, you need to follow up with people you meet at GDC so they become part of your network.

If you have a great conversation with someone about level design, but leave without exchanging information, then they can't help you later on, just as you can't help them. But, if you exchange information and follow up after, you at least create the possibility that one of you can impact the other in some beneficial way.

Fortunately, learning how to do this isn't that tough. Here's what a good sample networking scenario looks like:

You're sitting next to someone at a talk, waiting for it to begin.

You: Have you heard [the speaker's name] talk before?
Other person: Yes/No/Other option
You: [Comment on their response, offering your own thoughts]

You both have a short conversation on what both drew you to this particular talk.

You: [Ask what they do in games/where they work/their name]
Other person: [Responds]
You: [Tell them what you're interested in/your projects/etc]
You: [Ask if they have a business card]

If they have a card, exchange cards. If they don't have one, just give them one of yours.

You: [Continue conversation if desired, otherwise end it]

THIS IS CRITICAL! After the talk ends, write on the back of their card where you met and what you talked about.

A week or so after GDC ends, send them a follow-up email saying how good it was to meet them. Include a reference to where you met and what you talked about to help jog their memory. After you send the email, send them a LinkedIn invite.

The details will vary, but the important parts should always be the same:

1. **Ask** what they do in games
2. **Identify** things you can talk about/ways you could possibly provide value to each other
3. **Ask** for their card, and give them one of yours
4. **Write down** details of how you met to remind yourself later
5. **Follow up** after the conference

Avoid This Networking No-No
When networking, do not walk up to people, exchange business cards with them, and walk away. If you don't make a genuine attempt to connect with someone before giving them your card, they will most likely throw it away as soon as you're out of sight. The card is simply a reminder of the interaction you had with them. It cannot provide a meaningful interaction on its own.

Go to the Parties

Oh my, the parties. GDC has many parties.

You'll encounter several kinds of parties at GDC. Most of them will have open bars, or will at least be held at bars, so you will need to be 21+ to get into most of them.

While a few scattered parties happen on Monday night, the bulk of them happen between Tuesday and Thursday night.

Remember above all, you're at GDC to work at getting into the game industry and to make a good impression on everyone you meet. Make sure to know your limits and not get carried away drinking. One helpful practice is to drink a glass of water after every alcoholic beverage to keep you at an even pace.

Here's a basic breakdown of what to expect from GDC nightlife, using real examples from past conferences:

Party Type	Example	What to Expect
Huge Company Invite-Only Extravaganza	Microsoft or Sony renting a gigantic venue with a multi-floor setup	If you're not invited, you may not make it in. If you can find a way inside, the networking and amenities will be worth it.
Huge Company Party Fest	Notch's .party(), a massive rave featuring Skrillex	A crowded, feverish dance floor. Fun, but not good for networking.
Indie Game Party	That Party / Wild Rumpus, a venue with indie game installations and chiptune performances	Indie and mainstream developers with interesting games and prototypes set up for play. Good networking & vibes.
Game Industry Establishment Party	The IGDA's annual party	Pretty much the same feel of GDC, except at night and with drinks. Good networking but it usually ends early.
Crashable Mid-Tier Game Party	Adult Swim's party at Jillian's, the venue across the street from the convention center	If you can find a way in, you'll be rewarded with good networking and a fun bar-like atmosphere.
Well-Known Company's Recruiting Party	LucasArts' party at a nightclub	You can usually find out about these recruiting-focused parties by wandering through the career fair. Good networking, especially if you're interested in working at the company hosting.

Tiny Indie Studio Party	Wadget Eye's party at a bar	Smaller crowds mean a less intense atmosphere. You'll meet people involved with the host company, and with other small indies. Can be more intimate.
Media Outlet Party	Destructoid's party at a large venue	These are generally easier to get into, and a diverse crowd means good potential networking. Loud music may make conversation difficult, however.
Random Peripheral or Software Service Company You've Never Heard Of Party	A company you never heard of throwing a party a ~20 minute walk away from everything else	These can be hit or miss opportunities. Networking will be a total grab bag, so if things don't look promising, don't stay too long.

Finding Parties

There are a few ways to find out info about parties:

1. Talk to people.

When the daytime GDC programming stops around 5:00 PM, feel free to ask people if they know about any parties that night during your conversations. This is even better if you know at least one party, and you freely volunteer that information.

2. Go to the expo and career fair.

Some companies freely give out invitations to their parties during the day, then strictly turn people away at the door who don't have them. Doing a pass through the expo and career fair could put some invites in your pocket ahead of time.

3. Share with friends.

If you make any conference buds, let them know about parties you discover. You'll find that they'll be sure to share the wealth when they find out about other events.

4. Look online.

For a certain subset of GDC-goer, finding the parties is like a metagame within GDC itself. You can join the Facebook group, The Fellowship of GDC Parties, for a direct line to party time.

Reference Material [Link]
The Fellowship of GDC Parties Facebook Group:
https://www.facebook.com/groups/TheFellowshipOfParties

The Hiring Mindset

Whether you realize it or not, breaking into the games business is fundamentally a sales transaction. You are selling yourself, which is the combined package of your skills, experience, personality and potential, to someone who is looking to buy.

The person on the other end of the deal is, just like you, a person. Like you, they have a concrete goal they are trying to accomplish: To find someone to work on their game.

The mindset of this person is surprisingly clear. Here are the questions they'll be asking themselves throughout the process of meeting, interviewing, vetting, and discussing you with other people who have a stake in the hiring process:

1. Can this person do the job?
2. Is this person the best candidate we've found so far?
3. Can this person work well with our team?
4. [Classified]

1. Can this person do the job?

This is the qualifying round. If your samples/portfolio/test materials pass muster, and if you have the minimum amount of experience the hiring team is looking for (not just what they list in the job description), you'll be officially in the running and will be considered as an actual candidate.

If you're on the outside trying to break into the game industry, meeting this requirement is one of the hardest parts of the breaking in process.

2. Is this person the best candidate we've found so far?

You're past the first round of interviews, but now you've got competition. In order to move past this stage, you simply have to be better than everyone else in the running.

The good news is, it's pointless to compare yourself to any of your competitors. The way to progress here is to relentlessly focus on improving your own skills.

Show Your Learning Curve
Because game development is such a fast-paced activity, you'll need to be able to learn and master new tools, processes and concepts on the fly. For this reason, being a fast learner is an excellent trait to cultivate.

In your interviews, think about how you can demonstrate your ability to quickly learn new things, and be ready to get the point across.

3. Can this person work well with our team?

Does your personality gel with the team members? Does it seem like you can work well in the studio's existing culture? There's not as much you can do here, since to a large degree, team fit is based on personality.

This is something outside your control, so if you are turned down from jobs due to fit, take it as a sign that your skills are in the right spot. Factors beyond your control are influencing the decision here.

As a prerequisite for this requirement, you have to be able to work well in any team to begin with. Can you add value as a functioning member of a team? Do you know when to push back and when to accept compromise? Do you have a greater perspective of the company's goals, vision and capabilities, and your place as a contributor? The more experience you get working in collaborative settings, the better prepared you'll be in a real group development setting.

4. *[Classified]*

While you can boil down the hiring mindset to a few key points, there will always be mysteries that will never be made clear to you.

Were you given multiple indications that you were the best candidate and the gig was a shoe-in, only to never hear from anyone in the studio ever again? It's very possible that:

- The studio lost their funding
- The project's publisher backed out
- The tech/creative/audio/art lead quit, sending the department into disarray
- The studio lost a critical tax break, forcing waves of layoffs
- The offshore outsourcing studio where 80% of the work is done underwent a revolution/civil war/domestic attack, and all new projects are suspended indefinitely

Literally anything can happen, so there's no sense in worrying about events beyond your control. Keep this in mind during the interview process to help retain perspective.

"I always tried to find out why I wasn't chosen for a job so that I could apply that knowledge to my next attempt."
    —John McLean-Foreman
    Narrative Director/Lead Writer | Freelance

Help Them Mitigate Risk

You can't do much about points 3 and 4, but you can get into the game industry by making sure points 1 and 2 are locked down. The hiring mindset is all about **mitigating risk**. Will this person screw up if we hire them? Or will they be able to do the job, learn from challenges and do the best job possible?

Strive to minimize risk in the minds of the decision makers. Become the person who poses the least risk of screwing up and gives the most assurance of doing the best job possible.

How Do You Hire?

Evan Skolnick, Senior Writer | Telltale Games
"There are three aspects I generally look for. First and foremost, a high level of skill and ability in their chosen craft. If you're not actually good at the work itself, nothing else really matters.

This is followed by flexibility. Game development is incredibly dynamic and requires developers to not get overly attached to their ideas or prior work. Walking into work and finding out the previous day's efforts are now redundant and must be reworked is a common occurrence. Being able to bounce back from such frustrations and quickly start to attack the new problem is vitally important.

Finally, I look for someone who is a good collaborator; someone whom others will find they enjoy working with. With nearly all games being developed by cross-disciplinary teams, it's never been more important for a developer to play (and work) well with others."

John McLean-Foreman, Narrative Director/Lead Writer | Freelance
"To be honest, I don't hire junior writers anymore. It takes too much time to edit their work and train them, so I need people who are as good as me or better. That said, if I see that burning desire in an applicant to the point where they'll do whatever it takes to master the art form, then I'll take the risk and give them my time.

For those with more experience, I look for people who can handle criticism;

love the art form; are willing to collaborate; understand that no matter how amazing their idea, if it doesn't fit the game or story anymore, they need to throw it out; and are fun to work with."

Coray Seifert, Director of Production | Experiment 7
"Show me that you finished your own independent game and then sold it. Don't show me a half-finished project. Show me that you were an intern on a Halo or an Angry Birds or a VR prototype with Oculus and that you learned a ton from listening to everyone you could find. Don't show me a resume that has huge gaps in it or a resume with irrelevant experience. Show me that even if you worked on a level for a game that failed, you finished it all the way through, including optimization and performance profiling.

Above all, show me that you have energy, that you love games, and that you love the process of making games, not just the outcome of game development."

Which Do You Do?

At the beginning of Chapter 2, I asked a question:

Say, for example, there are only three ways to break into the game industry. One of them takes a significant amount of time, one of them costs a non-trivial amount of money, and one of them requires serious self-improvement. Which of them do you do?

Do you have your answer? The correct answer is **every one you can**.

Breaking into the game industry is incredibly competitive. Why on Earth would you not want to give yourself all of the advantages you can?

Chapter 4: You're In - Now What?

Your First Game Job

"I had to try basically every avenue of entering the industry until one worked."
—*Josh Raab*
Associate Game Designer | Big Huge Games

Congratulations! After an immense amount of hard work, sacrifice and effort, you've landed your first job in the game industry.

You wake up every morning with a crazy grin on your face as you head to work. During your first few weeks, you still can't believe that you're being led behind the scenes of game development. They're paying you to do this! It'll seem like a dream.

You'll surprise yourself with your enthusiasm. You'll jump at chances to learn about this and that, and to help out with whatever comes your way. At night, you'll think about ways to make the game better.

Make no mistake, your enthusiasm is well warranted. It'll serve you well in the initial ramping-up period. But make sure that you don't let your pure joy slowly creep into working 9, 10, 11-hour days of your own volition.

Because your true journey to the games industry is still far from over.

Breaking into games is a difficult thing, and you should be proud. Yet there's a reason why developers tend to leave the industry on a regular basis, and that reason is burnout. If you intend to stay in the game industry for the long haul, you'll need to make sure to not work yourself to exhaustion in your first few years on the job just because you get paid to work on videogames.

Make Your Mark, With Eyes Open

"Don't be afraid to take low level jobs and equally important, don't be afraid to leave them, especially if it turns into a bad situation. No bad situation is worth a completed credit for the damage it does to your health, your fitness for employment and your psyche."
—Raison Varner
Sound Designer and Composer | Gearbox Software

Your best strategy in your first game job is to learn as much as you can and be as proactive as possible, all while maintaining a sustainable working pace. There may come time to crunch on a game - especially near the end of a project - but if there is no external pressure to do so, prioritize keeping yourself well-rested and not overworked.

It's one thing to volunteer for assignments, do the occasional research over a weekend, or offer to help out with special projects. It's another thing to let yourself be exploited by management that can't plan correctly or doesn't want to pay overtime. It's a fine line, and as someone new to game development, you must be cautious to tread it carefully.

Be aware of how your studio's culture compares with other game companies'. During periods of intense work, it can be helpful to check in with friends and acquaintances at other studios to see how their work hours, use of overtime and general office cultures compare to yours. If you realize that conditions at your studio are significantly worse than others, it may factor into your decision to stay or leave for a new company. In general, avoid getting tunnel vision at your company, and never assume that conditions at your studio are the same everywhere.

Adjust Your Professional Expectations

If you're transitioning into games from a different industry, be prepared to adjust your salary expectations. Salaries are generally lower in games than in similar industries simply because of the competitive nature of getting into games.

Not only will you have to make peace with this fact, you'll also have to work extra hard to distinguish yourself as much as you can in order to gain more responsibilities and move up the ladder.

You'll also need to prepare yourself for a decrease in seniority. Game development is a very nuanced field that combines numerous technical and creative disciplines, and there are many parts to that process that you'll have to learn from the ground up. Even if you're coming from a storied career in your previous field, stay humble and keep your mind open. If you're able to immerse yourself and learn, your previous work experience will act as a multiplier in boosting you up the ladder.

If you're coming into games directly from school, it's a good idea to research average salaries for your chosen discipline in other industries to have a more objective idea of your value. This will help you make a case when asking for raises, and to help keep an idea of what realistic compensation should look like at different skill and experience levels.

For insight into what to expect from game development salaries, check out the salary surveys put out by Gamasutra and MVCUK:

Reference Materials [Reading]
Gamasutra 2014 Game Developer Salary Survey
http://www.gamasutra.com/view/news/221533/Game_Developer_Salary_Survey_2014_The_results_are_in.php

MVCUK 2015 Game Industry Salary Survey
http://www.mcvuk.com/news/read/how-much-are-you-worth-find-out-with-the-results-of-mcv-s-2015-salary-survey/0144271

For an insightful look into what you can expect working at a big studio, read this overview of a talk Bioware's James Ohlen gave on the realities of working at a large established developer:
http://www.gamasutra.com/view/news/281853/The_realities_of_being_a_game_designer_in_a_big_studio_like_BioWare.php

This blog post from former Ubisoft designer Maxime Beaudoin explains his motivation for leaving the studio and striking out on his own as an indie:
http://gingearstudio.com/why-i-quit-my-dream-job-at-ubisoft

Above All, Distinguish Yourself

There are concrete reasons you should be aiming to distinguish yourself from the get-go:

1. **Networking doesn't stop when you break in.** Having a strong network will help you get in the door, and it will sure as hell help you stay in. Your new coworkers are now some of your most important industry contacts. Why are they so important? Because when your studio closes or lays off staff and your former colleagues end up at dozens of other studios all over country or even the world, you'll have a direct contact on the inside.

2. **Collaboration breeds opportunity.** If you end up working really well with a coworker, it isn't too crazy to imagine the both of you working on a side project or two. Maybe it starts just as a hobby, maybe it leads to nothing… but it could also lead to other projects, other collaborators, and one day years down the line, you could find yourself starting a company with the people you once worked alongside in your first job. This is a timeless story throughout the industry.

For an example, read up on how Greg Kasavin's coworkers in his first associate producer job for EA ended up being his cofounders at Supergiant, creators of *Bastion* and *Transistor*: http://www.q-avenue.com/interview-with-greg-kasavin-of-supergiant-games

3. **You should want to.** If you're burning to work in the game industry, it would stand to reason that you're thoroughly excited about actually doing the work involved. The more you push to set yourself apart as an extraordinary contributor, the better you'll become at putting together successful games.

Your Second+ Game Job

"Pursuing a career in the games industry means accepting a layoff risk twice that of the national average (Gamasutra's Salary Survey 2014) and the likelihood of changing employers nearly three times every five years with 48% of unemployment periods exceeding 12 months (IGDA's Developer Satisfaction Survey 2015)."

—Evan Berman
Senior Community Manager | Bethesda Softworks

With a career in games, it's highly likely you'll end up changing jobs and moving to new cities at least a few times. The moving part can be mitigated somewhat if you live in a major game industry hub like LA, San Francisco, Austin or Montreal, but even then nothing is guaranteed. And though it's exceedingly rare, there is a small chance you could become one of the few to stay at the same studio for a number of years.

Since the odds are high that'll you be relocating at least once in your career, it makes sense to put the effort in to guide yourself through this transition on your own terms. Making smart lateral moves can be the difference between moving up the ladder in responsibilities, skill development and salary, and grinding out the same few rungs of the career ladder for years.

Here are some ways to prepare yourself in your journey up the ranks of game development:

1. **Trace your ascension.** Most disciplines follow the same basic arc from entry-level to mid-level to senior to director to executive. While you definitely don't have to climb to the highest level in order have a "successful" career in games, it helps to have an idea of what you want to achieve and what's possible.

In most companies, entry-level positions are at the assistant or associate level (Associate Producer), while mid-level titles lose the qualifier (Producer). At the higher levels, titles and responsibilities start to becomes less standardized (Lead/Senior Producer) as the specifics of what a role entails may differ significantly depending on the studio. Finally, the highest levels (Director of Production/Executive Producer) are generally concerned with managing departments, overall vision for a game or series, or strategic opportunities beyond day-to-day operations.

2. **Ask how to level up.** After enough time on the job to get comfortable with your responsibilities and to get an idea of what's expected of you to move up the ladder, ask your boss exactly what it would take to get you to the next level. You may not be eligible for a promotion anytime soon, but the answer they give you will be valuable information. And just by showing that you intend to put in the work to progress sends a clear signal about your work ethic and ambition.

On the other hand, the lack of a good answer can be equally informative and potentially serve as a warning. If management doesn't have a clear path for your career to grow, and there is no institutional process in place on promoting leadership from within, you may be left without any real clue on how far your career could realistically progress at your current company.

"The best way that I've found to keep moving up in the industry is through networking and paying your dues…you'll have to prove yourself through smaller and less well-known projects before contacts will be willing to book you on bigger and more important projects."
   —*Caitlin L. Conner*
   Lead Narrative Designer | Gameloft

3. **Start doing the next job before you get it.** The easiest way to get promoted is to start doing the job you want before you get it. Depending on how observant management is, getting the promotion in writing will simply be a matter of acknowledging the work you've already been doing. Of course, make sure not to step on any toes in this process. The key takeaway is to perform above your current position while still helping the company function. Serving your own ambition to the detriment of coworkers is an absolute no-no.

4. **Make lateral moves.** If it seems apparent that management has no intention of granting you the promotion you so obviously deserve, it might be time to start looking around at other studios. Not only are lateral moves to other companies a great way to negotiate a salary bump, but the more kinds of in-house production processes and techniques you can experience firsthand from different companies, the more valuable your experience in the industry will be. Learning from places that do some things badly and a few things right can be just as valuable as working somewhere that seems to do everything perfectly.

5. **Watch for danger signs.** Are there rumblings that your publisher is backing out of the project? Did your studio's last big release fail to hit sales targets? Did a remote office suddenly close, or a department suddenly lose a few team members? Keep an eye on anything that may portend rough times ahead for your company. If you think your studio may be preparing for layoffs or even a studio-wide closure, now may be the time to check in with your network for any possible open positions.

At the same time, don't let unfounded office gossip drive you into an unnecessary panic. Always respond to speculation with skepticism and wait for hard information before deciding how much you believe any given rumor.

Remember, if you get caught in a wave of layoffs, you'll suddenly be competing with your former coworkers for a limited supply of jobs at other studios. Be vigilant - your career may be at stake.

"Keep your resume updated on a quarterly or even monthly basis and acknowledge that your current company may not be your "forever" company."
   —Evan Berman
   Senior Community Manager | Bethesda Softworks

6. **Beware the crunch.** No matter the steps companies claim to take against it, crunch time is a fact of life in game development. It's highly likely that there will be times, either due to poor scheduling or

circumstances beyond the team's control, that you'll need to work long days and/or weekends, for weeks or months at a time.

Before you realize it, suddenly two months have gone by and you haven't seen any friends or family, you're eating terribly and have gained weight, and you're barely getting any sleep.

To prevent the effects of crunch from sneaking up on you, prepare yourself before it happens. Read up on some of the worst-case scenarios, so you know what is reasonable and what should not be tolerated. Get familiar with some of the precedents for QoL (Quality of Life) initiatives in the industry, and what people have had to contend with already.

Some recommended crunch-related reading:

Reference Materials [Reading]
A cautionary tale of the health risks of crunch:
http://www.gamasutra.com/blogs/KatherineRogers/20140403/214684/Working_in_the_Games_Industry_a_job_to_die_for.php

Read up on the "EA Spouse" saga that broached an industry-wide Quality of Life discussion:
Original post: http://ea-spouse.livejournal.com/274.html
Settlement: www.gamasutra.com/view/news/100005/Programmers_Win_EA_Overtime_Settlement_EASpouse_Revealed.php
The aftermath: http://www.gamesindustry.biz/articles/2013-03-28-ea-doesnt-get-enough-credit-says-ea-spouse

A critical read of a Blizzard recruitment video:
Video: https://www.youtube.com/watch?v=_9ng2EO_IKY
Article: https://www.pastemagazine.com/articles/2014/08/working-for-the-love-of-the-game-the-problems-with.html

"I was fortunate enough to have a long (eight-year) run at a single studio, but since then it's been a pretty rocky ride. My strategy was to

move my family and myself to an area with multiple game studios so that a change of jobs wouldn't necessarily require a change of location. It's worked out fairly well, but not perfectly. Instability is an inherent part of our industry, unfortunately."
 —*Evan Skolnick*
 Senior Writer | Telltale Games

Above all, realize that your game development career is yours to manage. For example, your company may make claims about how everyone in the studio is a family. Some studios may earnestly believe in that philosophy, and will strive to make sure employees are treated fairly and their voices are included.

However, most of the time, that's a phrase designed to subtly instill loyalty to the company and manipulate your sense of duty. Don't be fooled - game companies are notoriously unstable and layoffs are common. If phrases like "family" are used to try to cover up a toxic work environment, don't be afraid to push for reform or change jobs. Real family members don't fire each other.

Rather, never forget that every game company you work for is a for-profit business endeavor that will always fire staff if it means the company's survival. To ensure a long-term game industry career, you must always keep your best interests at heart.

"Be loyal to yourself and considerate of your company, not the other way around."
 —*Caitlin L. Conner*
 Lead Narrative Designer | Gameloft

Chapter 5: Conclusion

Play The Game

You've toiled through obscurity, educated yourself about the industry, immersed yourself in the rituals, built a network of like-minded adventurers, and found yourself employed in the game industry.

It's an ironic fact of videogame development that something that provides so much amusement for people can take such staggering amounts of work to produce. As you go to work, remember the joy that sparked you to take this journey.

Keep the sense of wonder with you, a constant reminder that the work you do is in service of creating more moments of amazement and otherworldly experiences for people just like yourself.

Take care of your mind, your body and your spirit, even during the darkest times you may encounter.

Don't forget to reach down to others who burn to take the same journey that you did. Stoke the fire in their belly. Push them to realize what exactly it will take to get there.

And once you've made sure that they know what risks, rewards and trials lie ahead - do your best to pull them up all the same.

Acknowledgements

This book is the result of years of firsthand experience working in games, but it wouldn't exist without the help of the many friends and collaborators listed here.

Big thanks to my family: my mom Naomi for understanding that all those marathon gaming sessions would serve a purpose someday, and for giving me my first glimpse of the game industry by taking me to Acclaim for a focus group for *Batman Forever*; my dad Lew for teaching me how to shoot, skate, score penalty shots and fight (conveniently all in *Blades of Steel*); and my sister Emily for sharing many childhood moments of soaring wonder and teeth-gnashing frustration (care of *Kirby's Adventure* and *Legacy of the Wizard*, respectively). Hooray for the treehouse!

Lots of gratitude to my fantastic girlfriend Katherine Moore for prodding me to finish this project, helping brainstorm a much better title, and generally having good ideas all the time. You're great and good and lovely and that's just how it is.

Thanks to everyone who read early drafts and gave feedback: Shuichi Aizawa, Caitlin L. Conner, Dennis Crow, Jess Fiorini, Dennis Liaw, Josh Raab, Coray Seifert, Lew Serviss, Naomi Serviss, Neil Sveri, Dylan Tredrea, Raison Varner, Andy Wallace. This text solidified into a far more complete resource thanks to your insight.

Thanks to all the game developers who took the time to be interviewed: Evan Berman, Caitlin L. Conner, Dennis Crow, Nick Madonna, John McLean-Foreman, Josh Raab, Coray Seifert, Evan Skolnick, Neil Sveri, Dylan Tredrea, Raison Varner. I know the next generation of game devs will be grateful for the wisdom you shared.

Thanks to the folks at Damonza for creating an excellent cover, and to Mitch Boyer, Chris Hernandez, Ken Inoue and Katherine Moore for feedback on the design.

Thanks to my game and writing mentor John McLean-Foreman for opening my eyes to the possibility of writing for games in the first place. You've made a world of difference, my friend.

Thanks to Coray Seifert for shepherding an ambitious but clueless college kid into the crazy world of game development. Your peanut butter-filled pretzels are en route.

Special thanks to the GDC CA community for their vibrant sense of community and unique perspective within the industry. See you in the lounge!

Thanks to everyone else who helped me break into games, and to everyone who I nudged along the same path, knowingly or unknowingly. We're truly in this together.

Finally, thank you for reading! If this book helps you or if you have any feedback, I'd love to hear it. Send me a note at ben@dashjump.com or find me on twitter at @benserviss.

Appendix A: Gameography

Here are all the games that I worked on for your reference.

Title	Role	Platform	Company	Notes
1. *Solarball*	Writer (Intern)	Web	OnlineWorlds	
2. *StarTrades*	Writer (Intern)	Web	OnlineWorlds	Ran 2004 - 2016 at startrades.com
3. US Military Training Simulation	Game Designer (Contract)	PC	Stottler Henke	
4. *TimeShift*	Associate Producer	360/PS3/PC	Saber Interactive	Released 2007
5. *Dragonica Online*	Product Manager	PC/Mac	THQ*ICE	Released 2010
6. *Vampire Diaries: Get Sucked In*	Writer (Contract)	Facebook	Arkadium	Released 2011
7. Gamified Retail Loyalty Program	Game Designer (Contract)	Mobile	Dopamine	Project for a major national retailer
8. Gamified Digital Currency App	Game Designer (Contract)	Mobile	Dopamine	Project for MintChip, Canada's digital currency
9. Mobile Game Prototype	Game Designer (Contract)	Mobile	The Grocery Game	
10. Gamified Mobile Payment App	Game Designer (Contract)	Mobile	Dopamine	Project for iOS app Mogl

11. Gamified Financial Education App	Game Designer (Contract)	Mobile	Dopamine	Project for a major national investment firm
12. Gamified Project Management Program	Game Designer (Contract)	PC/Mobile	Dopamine	Project for a major national bank
13. *Binary Tactics*	Game Designer (Contract)	PC/Web	AF Dudley	
14. *Past/Present*	Game Designer (Contract)	PC/Web	Center for New American Media	Released 2013 pastpresent.org
15. Medical Training Simulation	Writer (Contract)	PC	Kognito	
16. Gamified Political Network Experience	Game Designer (Contract)	Web	Polly	
17. *Shadows of Siren*	Game Designer (Contract)	Web	Creo Ludus Entertainment	Playable teaser released in 2012
18. *The Last Monster Master*	Developer & Writer (Contract)	Web/Mobile	Choice of Games	Released 2014
19. Gamified Motivational Program	Game Designer (Contract)	Web	Experiences Unlimited	
20. Branded Collectibles Game	Game Analyst (Contract)	Facebook	Deckdaq	
21. *Don't F**k Up*	Game Designer	Proprietary Touchscreen Table	Studio Mercato	Sold the game and IP in 2013
22. *Nika*	Producer	Mobile	Studio Mercato	Released 2016

| 23. *Crystal Brawl* | Game Designer, Producer | PC | Studio Mercato | Released 2016 |
| 24. *Hiveswap* | Writer (Contract) | PC | What Pumpkin Studios | In Development |

Appendix B: Game Developer Interviews

Evan Berman
Senior Community Manager | Bethesda Softworks
Highlighted Gameography: *Elder Scrolls Online, Quake Champions, Elder Scrolls: Legends, ArcheAge, Defiance, HAWKEN, TERA, Hellgate: London*

1. How did you develop the skills you needed to get your first job in games?

My first experience with community management was when IRC was beginning to be embraced by companies as cutting-edge technology for engaging with audiences. A television show, *Farscape*, held live chats after each episode premiered. When it was suddenly cancelled, I produced an online petition the same night that evolved into the Save Farscape campaign. As a result of collaborating with other community members, the grassroots movement led the Syfy channel to agree to a miniseries finale to properly wrap up the show.

Later in college, I interned at advertising firm Crispin Porter + Bogusky as part of a work-study program. Upon graduating with a double major in film and theatre production from the University of Miami, I accepted a job offer from the firm, joining as a video editor and developing my pre- and post-production skills producing commercials and brand essence videos. At the same time, I consulted for game fansites and published hundreds of articles for assorted games. About a year later, Flagship Studios offered me my first professional position where I was responsible for what I was already doing only in an official capacity.

2. What were the most helpful things you did to break into games?

As my path into the industry suggests, being proactive at the right time and in the right way makes all the difference when turning an interest into a career. After deciding on my desired role, I studied how community managers on games I played interacted with their audiences and discerned their best practices, improving upon them to hone their efficacy. Then I turned passion into action and committed myself to an announced cadence and standard of quality. When official representatives of my earliest communities noticed my voluntary efforts, the next step was establishing and maintaining lines of communication with the studio to build professional relationships and, in time, opportunities.

3. What's your process for learning new tools and staying current with new game development practices?

While community management's core tenets of retention and reacquisition remain constant, its skillsets and tools arguably change more often than any other game industry position. Ten years ago, a studio engaging with its community in the comments of a YouTube video was an innovative practice. Eight years ago, the same could be said for Facebook company pages. Seven years, Twitter. Jump forward to today and the same annual experimentation with and adoption of new communication platforms is still seen: Google+, Instagram, Twitch, SnapChat. While this focuses on social media networks, other practices such as data science and influencer relations have also been evolving over the last decade.

The best way to stay apprised of trends and avoid fads is to listen: to LinkedIn feeds, to your peers, and to your community. New disciplines such as livestream production are rapidly becoming a requisite skill for community managers and new tools that support them and provide actionable insights are constantly being developed. Experimentation is the best way to discern which practices are a good fit for my studio and its games. I research how each is utilized and performs, then try them out personally. After initial evaluation, if deemed a match for our efforts, I give it a trial run, monitor the results, and iterate or keep as tactic for future strategies.

4. How do you deal with the instability that can come along with a career in games?

Eight months into moving cross-country for my position at Flagship Studios, one of the co-founders knocked on the Marketing Team door and invited everyone to an unscheduled and mandatory company meeting. As you imagine, this became my first layoff experience and it wouldn't be my last. Pursuing a career in the games industry means accepting a layoff risk twice that of the national average (Gamasutra's Salary Survey 2014) and the likelihood of changing employers nearly three times every five years with 48% of unemployment periods exceeding 12 months (IGDA's Developer Satisfaction Survey 2015).

Unfortunately, risk is the name of the game but it does vary with company size and position seniority. Not unlike the volatility of Silicon Valley's technology startups, new and small studios carry the most risk but offer the highest reward. Conversely, large companies are more stable but compensation in the form of stock options or profit sharing is rare for junior roles. While this varies and each studio is different, the best practice is to remain vigilant but not let yourself overreact based on rumor or speculation. Keep your resume updated on a quarterly or even monthly basis and acknowledge that your current company may not be your "forever" company.

5. What advice would you have for people looking to break into games today?

Make manifest your passion! Show rather than tell. The first step is to identify what aspect of game development and publishing interests you most and matches your education or experience. The next stage is critical: do! If you want to be a level designer, design a level. Better yet, design an interactive demo of it using your favorite game's engine. Treat this as a hobby; getting skilled at anything is a marathon, not a sprint. With diligence, you'll have sufficient quality work to build a portfolio that demonstrates your ability.

Finally, find a studio that needs your selected role and market yourself to them as the perfect fit given your proven skills and enthusiasm. Visit the career pages of developers and publishers, reach out to third-party recruiters, and update your LinkedIn account regularly (if you haven't made one yet, open a new browser tab and do so right now). To modernize an adage from a bygone era, you're going to need to pound the digital pavement for work: positions that accept new talent with no work experience are in very high demand and competition for them will be fierce. You'll want to put yourself in the path of potential employers by attending conventions and asking about career opportunities at studios' booths. If you don't have them already, legible business cards with your contact information and LinkedIn URL on them are a critical must-have.

While searching, continue doing. Promote your voluntary work on your social media channels and call out the studios you're targeting. Make their most communicative staff aware of you so that when your resume hits their desk they already have a point of reference. Familiarize yourself with the company's latest developments and research their online communities to glean their game's key points of friction. Be ready to discuss these topics and, given the opportunity, present solutions that your desired position can perform to address them. In short, make the prospect of hiring you an easy decision for them: become a natural fit for their studio culture that fills an important company vacancy perfectly.

Caitlin L. Conner
Lead Narrative Designer | Gameloft
Highlighted Gameography: *The Blacklist: Conspiracy*, *Dragon Mania Legends*, *Order and Chaos 2: Redemption*

1. What made you decide to seriously pursue games as a career?

I've been playing videogames since I was a kid, but it didn't occur to me that I could seriously pursue it as a career until after I'd graduated college, and was lucky enough to be offered a part-time QA position by a friend I'd met while interning summers in high school at a company that produced casual games.

Initially I thought it would be a temporary job until I figured out what I wanted to do with my life, but while working there I had the opportunity to move from QA to a Project Manager role that also let me dabble in some creative work.

I learned from that experience that I really love the software production cycle, getting to grow content from a few initial kernels of an idea, and then iterating on it until it's ready for release. Game production is wonderfully challenging, creative, and collaborative work, and after experiencing it for the first time, I was totally hooked.

2. What were the hardest parts of breaking into games for you, and how did you overcome them?

The hardest part of breaking into games is landing that first job, so I was incredibly lucky to find contacts that helped me do that. From there, it's earning enough credits on games to keep leveraging your previous work to get more work, and then working on enough games that people have heard of to get picked for more, and more exciting projects.

The best way that I've found to keep moving up in the industry is through networking and paying your dues. The games industry is relatively small, so if you meet enough people they can then introduce you to other interesting people and opportunities.

It's also very important that you take advantage of the opportunities available to you, and not hold out for bigger and better projects right out of the gate. You'll have to prove yourself through smaller and less well-known projects before contacts will be willing to book you on bigger and more important projects.

3. How did you develop the skills you needed to get your first job in games?

I interned as a QA Tester for several summers in high school, then after I'd landed my first job doing that, I continued learning on the job to develop my other skills toward writing for games, as well as project management.

While it's true that you can formally study games, I think there's a lot to be said for it being an industry where the lessons you learn on the job are likely to be more valuable, as they train you how to manage what happens when something doesn't go as planned, and something always doesn't go as planned in games.

Part of the fun is finding creative solutions when you're under the wire, which often end up producing better product than what you'd initially planned.

4. What were the most helpful things you did to break into games?

Networking and recognizing how to package and market my accomplishments to gain the attention of future employers and contacts. When you're first getting started, the #1 most important thing you can do is attend events for your local games community, talk to people about the projects they're working on, and keep an ear to the ground for opportunities for which you might be eligible.

I've had really good luck with doing part-time QA work for various members of my local games community that helped me demonstrate my skills and reliability, and then had them refer me to their friends. Prior to landing that first full-time job in games, you will likely need to do some freelance work on a few projects to demonstrate to employers that they're hiring someone who already has the skills they're looking for.

5. What advice would you have for people looking to break into games today?

Study either art or programming. I'm proof that you can build a career in games without being skilled at either of these disciplines, but having at least a moderate level of skill at one of them will make you much more competitive in the jobs market. Particularly if you decide you're interested in becoming a Producer or Project Manager, having a general knowledge of programming will make you much more effective at your job. When the programmers encounter a problem, you're more likely to understand its fallout effects on the rest of your project, and be able to re-plan your schedule and asset allocation accordingly.

I would also advise you not to get discouraged too quickly. Attaining the level of success you wish for in games will require a lot of hard work and luck, but if you want it enough you can make it happen.

Dennis Crow
Game Director | Awol
Highlighted Gameography: *World of Warcraft, Grand Theft Auto V*

1. How did you decide what kind of work you wanted to do in games?

I'm still deciding! In my younger days, I was most helpful as a tester, and after that I went into production. Right now I'm a game director. As I continue to work in games, I try to follow my passion and help the team in as many ways as I can.

2. How did you develop the skills you needed to get your first job in games?

I developed the skills through playing games and being a huge fan. My first exposure to game development was participating in betas of Blizzard games like *Warcraft III* and *StarCraft*. Later on, when I got my first job on *Tony Hawk*, my thousands of hours of playing games meant that I could help a team right away as a tester.

3. What's your process for learning new tools and staying current with new game development practices?

I talk to friends, play games, and check blogs like Gamasutra. I also read a lot of non-game development books, where I learn a lot about life and human behavior that often can be applied to games and life in general.

4. What advice would you have for people looking to break into games today?

Start making games now. There's nothing stopping a young, hungry developer anymore. Amazing tools like Unreal, Steam, and Kickstarter make the barrier much lower than it used to be. Once you have made some smaller games, you will develop the skills that are useful on a larger game team. Developing these skills will also build confidence, which you'll need in your first job.

5. What do you look for in an entry-level new hire or project collaborator?

I look for someone who starts a lot of projects and is able to complete them. Ambition is great, and most ambitious people start new crazy projects. After that, I want someone who gets projects done, as that shows commitment and focus. The combination of ambition and focus is a powerful mix.

Nick Madonna
Founder/Business Development | PHL Collective
Highlighted Gameography: *F.E.A.R.*, *TimeShift*, *Halo: Combat Evolved Anniversary*, *Tom and Jerry: Colossal Catastrophe*, *ClusterPuck 99*

1. What made you decide to seriously pursue games as a career?

I was always fascinated with games but wasn't allowed to have any of my own until I was in high school. I would always play at a friend's house or arcade but never on my own television.

My parents wanted me to focus on schoolwork, art, and sports instead of playing games – which in hindsight was a brilliant call on their part but at the time I didn't understand the rationale. When high school rolled around I was allowed to get my first console, a Sony PlayStation. That console ultimately set me on my path into games. The more I played the more I started to study and learn about 3D art, animation and the game development process.

2. What were the most helpful things you did to break into games?

To boil that down into a one word answer? Risk. I learned that taking chances was the only way I was going to learn and evolve as a person and a developer.

Thinking back there are probably four major moments that helped me carve out my place in the industry: dropping out of college and transferring in my first year, moving to LA with shaky job security, taking a job in Saint Petersburg, Russia and leaving the AAA space and starting my own studio. Each of those moments have their own stories and lessons but each one is also rooted in the idea that I was in control of my future as long as I made decisions that would drive me forward towards something better.

3. How did you decide what kind of work you wanted to do in games?

I thought I decided what I wanted to do quite early in my career but that ended up evolving and taking different forms over time. My initial thought was to break in as an environment artist but that soon changed after I got into QA. I got a bulk of my experience in management from QA onward into Production. My critical path diverged from art into QA into production into studio management – and that's the simple version.

4. What's your process for learning new tools and staying current with new game development practices?

It's mainly been the same over the years – reading and keeping up to date with all things related to the industry. I read a lot every day. From game press to industry sites and everything in between, I set aside a good portion of my day to keeping up-to-date. In addition to that, the team at my studio keeps me on my toes with new tech and production pipelines.

5. What advice would you have for people looking to break into games today?

I think I covered some of this in a previous question but you need to be open to taking risks and diving off into the unknown. It might seem scary but it's the only way to learn and move forward. Taking on new experiences and soaking in knowledge from peers is more valuable than playing it safe and sitting at a desk cranking out annualized titles. Growing as a person and growing as a developer are one and the same. The more you take in from life, the more knowledge you can apply to your craft.

John McLean-Foreman
Narrative Director/Lead Writer | Freelance
Highlighted Gameography: *Killzone 3*, *Splinter Cell: Double Agent*, *Black & White 2*

1. What made you decide to seriously pursue games as a career?

Towards the end of the dotcom era I became an entertainment journalist of sorts. I specialized in doing 30-minute online audio interviews with just about anyone that I found interesting – it ranged from celebrities, to scientists, to video game developers.

I pursued that for a couple of years, but soon realized that I was always talking to people doing amazing things, but never creating anything myself.

I felt a burning need to build something, anything, and I foolishly thought that breaking into games would be much easier than film, so I left journalism and taught myself how to write stories.

I contacted every game company I could find and after two years of "No. No. No. Writers? Games don't need writers. No. No. Hey, I love that! But… uh… no.", I was becoming extremely frustrated. Even so, I knew that games held some great opportunity for me and I kept going until I got my first job as the lead writer on *Black & White 2*. (Incidentally, none of my story got into the final game).

2. What were the most helpful things you did to break into games?

One - I didn't really follow the traditional rules of conduct. I had a huge contact list for the game industry, so I would bypass whomever I needed to in order to speak directly to the decision makers. To be honest, I'm not really sure how good an idea that is, but back then it seemed to work.

Two – I found people whose opinions I valued that were willing offer honest critiques on my writing.

Three - I studied and practiced writing as often as I could.

Four – I applied to every single storytelling job that I could find in game development. Each application also required I complete a writing test, so that expanded my portfolio while also giving me practice at writing to a deadline.

Five – I always tried to find out why I wasn't chosen for a job so that I could apply that knowledge to my next attempt.

Six – Much to the annoyance of every girlfriend ever, I played LOTS of games. Now that storytelling in games is so much more advanced I would additionally advise that you keep a notebook beside you, pause regularly, and jot down what you feel does and doesn't work in your favorite games. You'll be amazed at what you discover.

Seven – I had a day job I HATED so deeply that no matter how exhausted I was by the time I got home, I was driven to write.

3. How did you develop the skills you needed to get your first job in games?

Back in my pseudo-journalism days, I had the good fortune of interviewing a comic book writer who was still pretty new to the scene: Brian Michael Bendis. At the end of the interview I asked him, "if you could recommend any book that teaches how to write, what would it be?"

Without hesitation, "Story by Robert McKee."

That book changed my life. I read it cover to cover multiple times, scribbled notes in the margins, read and dissected screenplays, taught other people how to write (that's one of the best ways to learn, btw), wrote stories that I would pay to see and play, submitted umpteen writing tests to every game company that would let me, and asked friends and colleagues to critique my work.

4. What were the hardest parts of breaking into games for you, and how did you overcome them?

One: The job I wanted didn't really exist.

While there were notable exceptions back when I began, most companies felt that having a writer on staff was unnecessary. I not only had to sell myself, I had to try to convince the execs that having a writer was vital.

I don't know that I overcame this as much as finally found a company that agreed with me.

Two: Dealing with rejection.

This part was unbelievably dispiriting. It was compounded by the fact that as the months turned into years, family, friends, and particularly my girlfriend all became more insistent that I start looking for other options.

I'm not sure why, but I had unswerving belief that I would find a way to break in. When I combined that with the worst day job ever, I was either going to succeed or throw myself in front of a train. Yeah. The job really was that bad.

5. What do you look for in a new hire or project collaborator?

To be honest, I don't hire junior writers anymore. It takes too much time to edit their work and train them, so I need people who are as good as me or better. That said, if I see that burning desire in an applicant to the point where they'll do whatever it takes to master the art form, then I'll take the risk and give them my time.

For those with more experience, I look for people who can handle criticism; love the art form; are willing to collaborate; understand that no matter how amazing their idea, if it doesn't fit the game or story anymore, they need to throw it out; and are fun to work with.

Josh Raab
Associate Game Designer | Big Huge Games
Highlighted Gameography: *Nika, Sumer, Crystal Brawl, DomiNations*

1. How did you develop the skills you needed to get your first job in games?

I've been designing games since I was a kid. Because I could barely code, I ended up making a lot of board and card games, which taught me the fundamentals of systems design. I learned other aspects of design, like creating mockups and maintaining documentation, while working on a number of solo and group projects in various contexts (internships, game jams, grad school, etc).

Programming is something I've slowly learned through classes and online tutorials - even though I'm a designer, having a little technical ability goes a long way. Other skills I use often in my current job are writing and research, which were part of my undergraduate education as a history major. I've also done sound design and project management for various games I've worked on. I picked those up almost exclusively through trial and error.

Finally, I overcame my personal awkwardness to become competent at meeting people at game industry functions, i.e. networking. This is a critical skill and not something that came naturally. I just put myself out there and eventually got better at it over time.

2. What were the most helpful things you did to break into games?

I'll start from where I am now and work backwards. I got my current job on a recommendation from Soren Johnson. He was the external advisor for my MFA thesis game, *Sumer*, at NYU Game Center. I was accepted into NYU partly because I was a regular at their playtesting events, where I got to prove my design skills by analyzing other people's games and showing off my own work. Many of the students and professors knew me, and I was at least a peripheral part of the community already.

More generally, I made games and met people. I took every opportunity to learn about and participate in the industry. One of my first short-term gigs was an internship for a video game PR company, Sandbox Strategies. I wasn't interested in PR, but one of the company's owners introduced me to an excellent NYC industry meetup group. I met a longtime collaborator posting about a board game on an NYU mailing list, long before I went to school there. You never know what will end up making a huge difference.

3. What were the hardest parts of breaking into games for you, and how did you overcome them?

I had to try basically every avenue of entering the industry until one worked. Even though I was fortunate enough to find an experienced freelance designer willing to take me on as an apprentice after my undergrad, I didn't make anywhere near enough to support myself with freelance work (and never have).

I published a board game, *Nika*, but found that board game designers only get a sliver of the profits. Between showing it at conventions and printing prototypes, Nika cost me far more than it will ever make me. My indie projects, while good practice and fun to work on, never showed any sign of providing a sustainable living.

The single hardest thing may have been dealing with the endless rejections and rejections-by-silence that came from sending applications to game companies. It always felt like a catch-22: you needed industry experience to get a job in the industry, which meant you couldn't get that experience in the first place!

Finding job openings and sending applications consumed a lot of time and energy and just felt like a huge waste. It was emotionally draining. Ultimately, the connections I made in grad school were the answer.

4. What's your process for learning new tools and staying current with game development practices?

I wouldn't say I have one. I've never been good about reading industry news or anything. I just pick stuff up as it becomes relevant to me.

I have at least read several game design books, including *Rules of Play* and *The Art of Game Design*. I also attend GDC (the Game Developers Conference) and watch talks online in the GDC Vault.

5. What advice would you have for people looking to break into games today?

Practice your skills and make connections. You need both skills and connections to have a shot. Sadly, I have found that the odds of getting a job through a regular application are abysmal when you have no experience. If you know someone who can recommend you, and you've proven yourself to be someone worth recommending, that'll likely be how it happens.

Don't be afraid to pursue things that aren't exactly what you want. If I had turned up my nose at doing PR, I might never have found that meetup group. If I refused to work on a free-to-play mobile game, I wouldn't have my current job. On the other hand, do keep your eyes on the role you ultimately want. You can "pivot" but you have to actively make it happen.

Finally, while I personally believe you should study something else in undergrad, I do recommend attending grad school for games if your career needs a push. You can learn a lot and make great connections. It worked for me and a lot of my classmates!

Coray Seifert
Director of Production | Experiment 7
Highlighted Gameography: *Magic Table* Series, *Homefront*, *Frontlines: Fuel of War*

1. What were the most helpful things you did to break into games?

I worked on everything I could get my hands on. Mods, puzzle games, indie projects, anything. Whether it was paying, sweat equity, internship, whatever.

Early in your career, you need to create at a ferocious pace. It might not be perfect, because you're just starting out. If you're extremely talented or lucky, you may end up working on something great. If you don't, that's fine. Going through the process of creating anything will set you miles apart from the mass of people who are afraid to get their hands dirty with something less than their perfect vision of what a game is. Get out there and create anything while constantly striving to get better at your craft. The quality will come with time and repetition.

For me, that meant making levels, game design documents and writing scripts that weren't perfect, but it was an important first step in my game development career.

2. What were the hardest parts of breaking into games for you, and how did you overcome them?

The hardest part was the sense of uncertainty. Looking back, I spent about two years breaking into the games industry by working on mods, independent puzzle games, and a highly experimental MMO. I thought I would never make it. The sense of dread was absolutely crushing, because when you're in the moment you don't know how your story is going to end; you don't know that you're working towards a certain goal.

Looking back, it wasn't much time at all in the grand scheme of things and I had a blast doing it. If I had known then what I know now, I would have enjoyed the process more and worried about the result less.

The way to overcome that sense of dread was just to be a relentless optimist, which can be a valuable tool when working in the games industry.

3. How did you go about building your portfolio, and how useful was it in getting into the industry?

I worked as a level designer on a number of ambitious but somewhat over-scoped mods. Looking back, my portfolio was…not great. That said, it was something and something is infinitely better than nothing.

I made sure that every project I worked on, I took away one great screenshot, game design document, or scriptwriting sample. Prospective employers liked that I had the initiative to find a team, learn new tech, and finish anything, even if it was not quite at AAA level yet.

This portfolio was the only thing that got me a job in the industry. It's fine to list "Game Designer" or "CEO" of your startup on your resume, but if you don't have anything to show for it, it's very difficult to break into the industry.

4. How did you develop the skills you needed to get your first job in games?

Mostly through learning through iterative design. I wrote tons of scripts, made tons of levels, and wrote tons of game design documents for projects that went nowhere. Each time, I was my own harshest critic and as I worked, I got better.

The saying "The master has failed more times than the beginner has tried" is super relevant here (and I say that as someone still embracing the path to mastery). Don't be frustrated by failure. Embrace it. LEARN from it. Constantly improve. Be happy with your work but never be content. Fail fast and happily move on to the next thing.

5. What do you look for in an entry-level new hire or project collaborator?

Anything real. Show me that you finished your own independent game and then sold it. Don't show me a half-finished project.

Show me that you were an intern on a *Halo* or an *Angry Birds* or a VR prototype with Oculus and that you learned a ton from listening to everyone you could find. Don't show me a resume that has huge gaps in it or a resume with irrelevant experience. Show me that even if you worked on a level for a game that failed, you finished it all the way through, including optimization and performance profiling.

Above all, show me that you have energy, that you love games, and that you love the process of making games, not just the outcome of game development.

Evan Skolnick
Senior Writer | Telltale Games
Highlighted Gameography: *The Walking Dead: A New Frontier*, *Mafia III*, *Gunship Battle 2 VR*, *Star Wars Battlefront*

1. What made you decide to seriously pursue games as a career?

It wasn't so much a plan or intention as something that just happened. I worked in traditional entertainment publishing such as comic books for quite a few years, then interactive development after that (websites, CD-ROMs, etc.). Transitioning from those into game development was just another phase that seemed to make sense for me, especially since I had already been a long-time game player.

2. What's your process for learning new tools and staying current with new game development practices?

As a writer in games this isn't a huge issue for me, though I do make sure to play or at least watch playthroughs of the latest narrative-driven games out there, to see how others are pushing this aspect of the medium forward.

3. What do you look for in a new hire or project collaborator?

There are three aspects I generally look for. First and foremost, a high level of skill and ability in their chosen craft. If you're not actually good at the work itself, nothing else really matters.

This is followed by flexibility. Game development is incredibly dynamic and requires developers to not get overly attached to their ideas or prior work. Walking into work and finding out the previous day's efforts are now redundant and must be reworked is a common occurrence. Being able to bounce back from such frustrations and quickly start to attack the new problem is vitally important.

Finally, I look for someone who is a good collaborator; someone whom others will find they enjoy working with. With nearly all games being developed by cross-disciplinary teams, it's never been more important for a developer to play (and work) well with others.

4. How do you deal with the instability that can come along with a career in games?

It hasn't been easy! I was fortunate enough to have a long (eight-year) run at a single studio, but since then it's been a pretty rocky ride. My strategy was to move my family and myself to an area with multiple game studios so that a change of jobs wouldn't necessarily require a change of location. It's worked out fairly well, but not perfectly. Instability is an inherent part of our industry, unfortunately.

5. What advice would you have for people looking to break into games today?

Make games with others as soon as you can, as it's the only way you'll really start to learn what's involved and why it's important to rein in project scope and everyone's expectations. Whether it's via a game program in high school or college, or just informally with friends, get experience making actual games as part of a team.

Also, network! Your network in the industry can be everything. Attend the Game Developers Conference (GDC) in your area if at all possible, and do your best to make industry connections there. Trying to break into a game studio through the front door can be extremely challenging if you don't know anyone at all on the inside.

Neil Sveri
Programmer and Co-Founder | DreamSail Games
Highlighted Gameography: *Don't F**K Up*, *Blade Ballet*

1. How did you develop the skills you needed to get your first job in games?

I'm self taught! I first tried programming in Python back in high school, fell in love with it, and then almost immediately found myself trying to make dumb little text games. From there, it was just learning and practice non-stop.

One of the biggest motivators for my work is learning, so a lot of my practice would just be to answer a single question like "How do projectiles work?". I also started doing game jams and developer meetups as often as I could, at first online and then in-person when I moved to NYC. Game jams were especially fantastic because they gave me incentive to work, had me meeting more experienced people, and would often result in me having a somewhat complete game at the end.

Doing all that brought me to where I am today, but I still try to spend time learning new things and practicing. It never ends!

2. How did you go about building your portfolio, and how useful was it in getting into the industry?

I hadn't released any projects when I was hired [at DreamSail], so I had to rely on my own personal experiments and demos. So since I didn't have the strongest body of work, I had to present it well and prove that, even with no releases, I knew what I was doing.

I decided to present the bulk of my work as screenshots and videos. Part of this was linking my Twitter, where I had been posting a huge amount of my work and process (Vine still existed at the time and was a great medium for small clips). Games that I had time to polish I packed as both executables and source code, with the idea to let them see both my programming and game design skills. In the end it payed off.

My producer, who hired me, said that he spent 45 minutes playing one of my small demos, and was impressed by a video of a flight game I made (I was brought on to make a flight racing game). So in the end, even though I had zero professional experience and zero released games, I focused on making my vast array of experiments available and accessible, and it managed to impress.

3. How did you decide what kind of work you wanted to do in games?

An interesting question because before I started programming I wanted to be a 3D animator. I would try to learn it and practice, but it never really clicked for me. Programming, on the other hand, clicked almost immediately. It's a kind of a mystery why one worked out better than the other. I might have simply had the aptitude to be a programmer, and because it came easier than art, I naturally wanted to pursue it.

I guess the blunt way to put it is that I decided to go into programming because I found that I was good at programming.

4. What's your process for learning new tools and staying current?

Like I mentioned earlier, my process for learning new things often involves answering a question. One of my favorites was "How does *Rocket League* render grass?" which burned a whole weekend of sleep on making awful, but educational, grass renderers.

With broader things, like an engine or workflow, I just dive in with the intention of making a specific thing. When I was learning Unreal, I set a goal to make a Planet Renderer. This is a somewhat complicated thing to do in a new engine, but in bite-size segments it really let me learn the engine. That often works better for me than following a step-by-step "Getting Started" tutorial.

As for how I stay on top of the industry, I'd say Twitter is a great resource. It provides a constant source of inspiration, news, and discussion from a large community of game developers. Sites like Gamasutra, Polycount, and TIGsource often link industry news and tutorials. I also like to join IRC and Slack groups for certain things, like a Unity Engine chat or a group for tech artists. They provide front-line news and somewhat intimate access to industry developers.

5. What advice would you have for people looking to break into games?

I think the biggest roadblock for people trying to get into the industry is their own apprehension. I've met plenty of people with the excuse of "I just don't know how to start". The best way to start is to start. The best way to learn how to make games is to make games. That sounds unhelpful but it's the truth.

Just sit down, download a game engine, pick apart the examples, read the documentation, and then try to make something happen yourself. The excuse holds up even less today because of all the resources for learning that exist, as there are courses and tutorials for every major tool and every major skill set. The scariest thing is getting started, but then everything else is a positive feedback loop.

Learning a basic thing will make more complex things accessible, and development will be more fun as you pick up more skills. So my advice is to just get started and don't stop.

Dylan Tredrea
Product Manager | Rovio
Highlighted Gameography: *Angry Birds Evolution, Angry Birds Action, Star Wars Assault Team, Nemo's Reef*

1. How did you decide what kind of work you wanted to do in games?

Marketing is where I started in games but frankly it wasn't very interesting to me. I just knew I was more of a businessperson than a creative so it seemed like a good place to start. When free-to-play, and in particular live operations of games as a service came along, I instantly knew Product Management was the job for me though.

While I understand that many people don't like the business side of things, I personally see it as where the most interesting challenges and opportunities are. Deciding which feature or game to prioritize over others is what often makes or breaks a game or a studio and the day-to-day process of how to run a live game is incredibly interesting. For me it's like a real time strategy game. "The game of games" is what I call it.

2. What were the most helpful things you did to break into games?

Make mods with friends. It was actually a horrible process and it's a miracle our friendships survived, but it was where I got a lot of rookie mistakes out of the way. It also undoubtedly gave me "street cred" when applying to real game studios without any "real" shipped games for positions that required game dev experience.

3. How did you develop the skills you needed to get your first job in games?

Probably one of the most pivotal jobs I had was in user acquisition at a Facebook slots developer. I had learned the basics at web startups doing similar work, but mostly I learned about the basics of how that works as well as the fundamentals of statistics and business from reading what other professionals were doing. It took some work to sift through the SEO BS, but there are plenty of top people who write and share what they know online if you make the effort to seek them out.

4. What advice would you have for people looking to break into games today?

Make games. It's so freaking easy with Unity, GameMaker, etc. You have no excuse. The point is not to make the next *Minecraft* by yourself. The point is to go through the process and finish something so you learn, harshly, how incredibly difficult the process of game development is and how incredibly worthless ideas alone are.

5. What do you look for in a new hire or project collaborator?

- If at all possible, has shipped a game (or even a mod) with a team of others
- Loves to debate stuff and isn't ever a jerk in disagreements
- Respects leadership and structure so if they "lose" an argument they just move on to the next thing
- Crazy curious, reads a ton, and always trying to learn stuff even if it's not related to work
- An analytical approach borne of humility: "While it is easy to lie with statistics, it is even easier to lie without them" and "All models are wrong, but some are useful" kind of attitude

Raison Varner
Sound Designer and Composer | Gearbox Software
Highlighted Gameography: *Prey, Red Faction: Guerrilla, Brothers in Arms: Hell's Highway, Borderlands, Borderlands 2, Tales from the Borderlands, Aliens: Colonial Marines, Battleborn*

1. What made you decide to seriously pursue games as a career?

Two soundtracks: The orchestral score to *Dark Wizard* (Sega CD) and a live orchestral soundtrack from *Final Fantasy 6*, that at the time was only available as an import from Japan. *Dark Wizard*'s soundtrack was so far ahead of its time. At a time of Genesis and SNES pixel graphics, this game came with a beautifully recorded live orchestral score. Most games today still don't come close to the quality of orchestration in *Dark Wizard*.

2. What were the most helpful things you did to break into games?

Work on mods and indie teams. Meet up with equally passionate and serious people in IGDA chapters to build games while in school or trying to break in.

3. What were the hardest parts of breaking into games for you, and how did you overcome them?

Deciding to avoid debt by not going to college put a large burden on me to educate myself. Beyond that, I think most people can get into the industry if they are willing to keep plugging away at it and have good skills. Don't be afraid to take low level jobs and equally important, don't be afraid to leave them, especially if it turns into a bad situation. No bad situation is worth a completed credit for the damage it does to your health, your fitness for employment and your psyche.

4. How did you develop the skills you needed to get your first job in games?

I don't think there's a substitute for working on small student or indie projects. You learn the terminology, the development process and it lends you credibility by having a shared language about development during interviews. If you can talk shop, you'll be in very good standing for any entry level job and you probably won't have released a commercial game in the process.

5. What's your process for learning new tools and staying current with new game development practices?

To be honest, game specific practices in development haven't really changed much in the 10 years I've been in the industry. The tech changes from time to time and there's more visual scripting than before, but it's all the same problems really. Staffing increases and new facilities have had a much greater effect on pushing oneself to improve or get left behind. Once you've solved the same problem in a game a few times (or a few different ways), your understanding becomes a little more agnostic from any specific engine.

www.ingramcontent.com/pod-product-compliance
Lightning Source LLC
Chambersburg PA
CBHW030759180526
45163CB00003B/1089